SLAUGHTER
on the OTTER

∿ —————————————————— ∿

The Kendrick Sheep Raid

Forest B. Dunning

ISBN: 978-1-59152-238-6

For more information or to order extra copies of this book call (you can add your own information here if you want) Farcountry Press toll free at (800) 821-3874.

sweetgrassbooks
an imprint of Farcountry Press
Produced by Sweetgrass Books
PO Box 5630, Helena, MT 59604; (800) 821-3874;
www.sweetgrassbooks.com

The views expressed by the author/publisher in this book do not necessarily represent the views of, nor should be attributed to, Sweetgrass Books.

Sweetgrass Books is not responsible for the content of the author/publisher's work.

Produced and printed in the United States of America.

23 22 21 20 19   1 2 3 4 5

No book with a historical bent can be written without the assistance of others. So it was with this book. Given the limited amount of public information on the Bear Creek (Kendrick) Sheep Raid, information had to be pieced together one bit at a time from widely diverse sources. The list of contributors to this story was many and varied.

I received valuable input from many people in the Birney and Otter communities of Montana in the form of oral history and stories from the time of their grandfathers and great-grandfathers. Specifically, the Brewster, Brown, and Alderson families from Birney were very forthcoming with old photographs and stories. "Bunny" Hayes and "Irv" Alderson were particularly helpful in putting the story in its historical context. In Otter, Marcus Stevens spent several hours with me traveling throughout the area pointing out important sites related to the sheep killing. His insight into the history of the Circle Bar Ranch and Levi Howes was critical to the confirmation of critical aspects of the story. Wally Badgett, Frank Hagen, Hardy Tate, Bill McKinney, the Bull family, and the Fletchers were all valued contributors.

One of the best informants with specific and valuable information was Neil Thex, grandson of Charles Thex, who spent hours researching the activities of his grandfather and the Bear Creek Raid. Without his help and encouragement, this book could not have been written.

Institutional assistance in Wyoming was provided by Cynde Georgen of the Trail End Museum in Sheridan, the Sheridan County Fulmer Public Library's Wyoming Room, the Sheridan Episcopal Church, the Washakie Museum & Cultural Center in Worland, and the American Heritage Center in Laramie; and in Montana, the Montana Historical Society Research Center in Helena, the Powder River Historical Society and Museum in Broadus, and the Range Riders Museum in Miles City.

A special thanks should go to John Davis of Worland, Wyoming, for his information and assistance on the Spring Creek Raid. I liberally used his research in the comparison of the Bear Creek (Kendrick) and Spring Creek Sheep Raids.

Most honorable mention should go to Alice Orr, English professor from Eastern Tennessee University, and Katie Curtiss, former history professor at Sheridan Junior College, for their good efforts to edit my abysmal spelling, punctuation, and historical references. They vastly improved the story.

Last, but most important, was the help of my son, Shane Dunning, who acted as my research assistant, mentor, editor, and chief critic. Without his great computer skills; hours of online time plowing through historical newspapers, census reports, obituaries, and court records; and recovery of hours of taped transcripts from long-dead pioneers, the book would never have been completed. In addition, his ability to recover old photographs and correctly size and caption them added immeasurably to the final work.

That I am still married is a tribute to my wonderful and loving wife, Susie, who put up with my frustrations, temper tantrums, and bad language over the past year.

TABLE OF CONTENTS

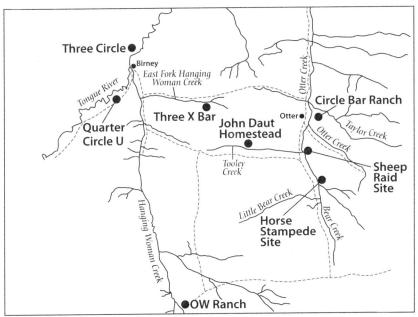

Figure 1: Map of the Otter Creek Valley Sheep Raid Sites.

UNDER THE TABLE

On a warm summer evening in 1956, I chanced to overhear the story that is related in this book. At the time I was only nine years old and staying for a few days with my step-uncle John Moreland at his ranch on Cook Creek in the Birney, Montana, area.

On that evening Uncle John was talking to an old cowboy about the days when he was a young man. A bottle of Old Hermitage whiskey was on the table, and they were both partaking liberally. The old man was J. H. "Shorty" Caddel, an old cowboy who had come "up the trail" and had worked at the Quarter Circle U Ranch at the beginning of the twentieth century. Shorty was only about five feet, five inches tall but rather heavyset. I recall that I was impressed that he was missing two fingers on his "dally" hand, and had tobacco juice running down one side of his chin and whiskey down the other side. He looked like he was the real deal. Since I had a keen interest in hearing old stories, I curled up under the table and listened intently.

The conversation began with Shorty describing how they worked the longhorn cattle on the open range and the trip up the trail from Texas. He talked about the problems that Birney and Otter Creek ranchers encountered with Cheyenne Indians killing their cattle because they were starving on the Cheyenne Reservation. He also gave his opinion of some of the local early settlers like John B. Kendrick, Captain Joseph T. Brown, George Brewster, Booker Lacy, and Levi Howes. At one point, after several drinks, Uncle John asked, "What do you know about that big sheep killing over on Otter Creek?" Shorty took some time to answer but then replied, "I was there. Guess I can talk now since I already told Lyman Brewster about it last year."

The tale that he told Uncle John that night has remained seared into my memory for over sixty years.

While doing research on another book, *Between Two Tribes*, I was visiting with an old army friend, Neil Thex, who grew up on Otter Creek, and mentioned to him that I remembered Shorty Caddel telling John Moreland that Charlie Thex, his grandfather, had been a participant in the sheep raid. Neil told me that he already knew about the raid because Lyman Brewster had written an article on the subject for the Montana Historical Society. Furthermore, he had a copy, which he mailed to me in addition to other information on his grandfather. Upon reading the article, memories came flooding back as the story I had heard was put in its historical context and filled in with the names of the other participants. However, because I was busy with the *Between Two Tribes* project, which was set in the year 1890, and the raid happened in late December of 1900, I had to defer action on the Bear Creek Raid until the first project was finished.

In my research on the first project, more information on the incident was uncovered. Again, I put that information aside until I could give it the attention it deserved. However, I noted that many of the players in the first book were also involved in the Bear Creek Raid.

Since the beginning of 1901, the "raid" has been variously named the "Kendrick Raid," "Otter Creek Valley Sheep Killing," and the "Bear Creek Sheep Raid." All are the same incident. Prior to 1974 the leadership of John B. Kendrick in the raid was not confirmed, and it was called the Bear Creek Raid. This book uses "Kendrick Raid" and "Bear Creek Raid" interchangeably.

It was terribly difficult to get accurate information about the Bear Creek Raid. While the topic has been awash with rumors for over 100 years, the only written material from the time are a few newspaper accounts, which are largely inaccurate. The most reliable sources are the interviews in the 1940s by Maude Beach of the Works Progress Administration, the Lyman Brewster article "December 1900: The Quiet Slaughter" published in 1974 in *Montana: The Magazine of Western History*, and various tape recordings of pioneers made by Robert Helvey in the late 1950s and 1960s.

Despite the difficulties, I believe that there is enough information to paint a reasonably accurate portrait of the raid—who planned it, who conducted it, and who helped cover it up.

The purpose of this book is to discuss the historical forces that led to the raid, record the facts, introduce the participants, describe their motivations, and assess the results of the raid. To some extent many of the conclusions reached are speculative in nature due to lack of verifiable information but reflect my best efforts to tell the story from the limited information available.

As of December 28, 2018, the raid occurred 118 years ago, and the participants are all long dead and buried. Over fifty years have passed since the last participant, Shorty Caddel, passed away on May 21, 1966. To those descendants who may feel offended by the exposure of the actions of their great-grandfathers in this book, I extend my sincere apologies. It was a different time and a new reality for those pioneer settlers who had to fight weather, grasshoppers, hostile Indians, outlaws, and then deal with hundreds of settlers out to secure their idea of the "American Dream." They made the great country that we now enjoy. Let us record this incident to the best of our ability and enjoy the courage and fortitude of our forbearers.

Here is the story as best as I can determine it.

Figure 2: Shorty Caddel and John Moreland, courtesy of Sharon Moreland Carleton.

CHAPTER ONE

THE RAID
Just the Facts Ma'am

As daylight broke on the morning of December 28, 1900, eleven men rode down a tributary to Otter Creek in southeast Montana on a grim mission. Their objective was the elimination of a band of sheep that had "invaded" their range six weeks earlier. Despite repeated warnings by cattlemen in the area, the sheep owners had taken the strictly legal position that the country was public land and they had as much right as the cattlemen to graze their sheep in that area. However, their actions ran counter to range customs that had been observed for many years, which delineated areas for sheep from those for cattle. This open violation of "range orders" was a potential death sentence to the cattle industry in the Otter Creek, Hanging Woman, and Tongue River drainages. When faced with the potential loss of homes and ranches, these cattlemen were prepared to take drastic action.

The riders were later identified by Lyman Brewster and Shorty Caddel as cattlemen John B. Kendrick, George Brewster, Charles Thex, Horton Boal, and Frank "Booker" Lacy and cowboys "Barney" Hall, William "Bill" Munson, Walt Snider, Mahlon "Tug" Wilson, Frank McKinney, and J. H. "Shorty" Caddel. At the junction of Tooley Creek and Bear Creek, they observed a sheep wagon, small corral, and about 2,200 head of sheep belonging to a partnership between John Daut and R. R. "Bob" Selway.

Figure 3: Site of the Bear Creek Sheep Raid, photo taken March 2018.

Donning gunnysacks with eye sockets cut out, they rode into herder Dan Squires' camp with ash clubs and guns in hand. One man, later identified as Charlie Thex, dismounted and, placing a pistol under the sheepherder's nose, said, "A little coffee, please. A little sugar, please."[1]

The remainder of the men dismounted and drank hot coffee after their cold ride. Following the coffee, they tied the sheepherder to his sheep wagon and proceeded to beat to death his 2,200 head of sheep. It should be noted that during the incident, the herder was not roughly treated or abused other than the indignity of being shown a gun and tied to a wagon wheel on a cold day in December.

Killing the sheep took most of the day and was incredibly hard work. There is some evidence that initially the men tried to kill the sheep in a roundup corral while on horseback.[2] However, the corral

---

[1] Shorty Caddel interview with Bob Helvey. Also Shorty Caddel with John Moreland and Forest Dunning.
[2] *Forsyth Times*, January 8, 1901.

was too small to hold 2,200 head of sheep, and it was difficult to hit a sheep perfectly from a moving horse in the middle of more frightened sheep. The corral soon became clogged with dead and injured sheep. The sheep were then pushed into a sharp bend in Tooley Creek underneath the high cut bank (shown on page 2). Because most of the dead sheep were found in this area, it was reported that the sheep were stampeded over the cut bank to their death.[3] However, this was not true. Almost all the sheep were killed by being clubbed in the head.

This particular herd was not made up of mature sheep. Instead it was a band of "coming yearling" ewe lambs that had been picked as elite replacements for Selway's other herds, as they were to be culled for age.[4] Because their skulls were not yet mature, these lambs were much more susceptible to death by clubbing than older sheep.

Following the dispatch of the sheep, the herder, Dan Squires, was untied and told to stay in camp for an hour. He was also instructed to leave the area or he would be killed on sight.[5] The sheep killing party then split up and returned to two separate ranches where they would be witnessed at New Year's weekend dances. On the way home, some of the men fell in behind wild horses and drove them in front to hide their tracks.[6]

The herder went to John Daut's homestead and reported the slaughter. He thought he recognized the voices and mannerisms of some of the raiders despite the gunnysack masks and told Daut who he suspected. Then Squires left Daut's house. He showed up at Captain Joe T. Brown's ranch on the Tongue River the next morning to report the raid. He went to the Three Circle Ranch because he had served under Captain Brown in the Montana State Militia and felt safe there.[7] He then departed for

3 *The Sheridan Post*, January 3, 1901.
4 Booker Lacy interview with Robert Helvey.
5 Shorty Cadell discussion with John Moreland and Forest Dunning, 1956.
6 Brewster, "December 1900: The Quiet Slaughter."
7 Arthur Hayes, Jr. (great-grandson of Captain Joe T. Brown) interview, March 2018.

unknown parts and was never seen in the immediate Otter Creek country again.

The following morning, John Daut came down Tooley Creek and found the dead sheep and abandoned sheep wagon. Proceeding on up Bear Creek, he informed the large flock herders of the raid. Then he rushed to the nearest telephone at the post office located at the Charles Bull ranch and called Custer County Sheriff O. C. Cato in Miles City to report the dead sheep and missing herder. While herder Squires had told Daut that he was leaving the country, Daut did not know where Squires was at the time of the report. Daut also sent word to St. Labre Mission at Ashland to tell the Northern Cheyenne tribe: "Heap big kill, bring plenty wagons."

Cato telegraphed the news to R. R. Selway in Sheridan, Wyoming, and then left for Tooley Creek. Selway immediately responded by offering a $2,000 reward for information relating to the killing.

Sheriff O. C. Cato made a quick investigation of the site, talked to John Daut, gathered several blood-stained clubs, and returned to Miles City to confirm that 2,113 sheep had indeed been killed by persons unknown.

Selway perceived that Cato was not all that interested in capturing the sheep killers after he told Selway, "I stand ready to arrest any man who comes in to claim his club."[8] Cattlemen from all over the county showed up at his office during the next month to examine the clubs. Joking comments like "I don't see my club here, mine had a knot in it," and "That looks like Joe's club but he was in your jail that night" were prevalent. When questioned by Cato, Shorty Badgett of the Bug Ranch said, "Are my initials on that club? I always put my initials on my clubs. If my initials aren't on it, must not be my club."[9] Most of the cattlemen thought it was a fine piece of work. Sheriff Cato was the former manager of the

---

[8] Brown and Felton, *Before Barbed Wire.*
[9] Interview with Wally Badgett (great-grandson of Shorty Badgett), May 10, 2018.

huge XIT cattle ranch and a lame duck, with only a month left to serve on his term.

Excitement abounded throughout the Otter and Birney communities as people wondered who had carried out the raid. Most of the prime suspects were those cattlemen and their cowboys in the immediate area. However, all had been seen at the dances held over the New Year's weekend. It was reported that Charlie Thex played the violin at one dance, and John B. Kendrick was much in evidence as he greeted guests at the OW.[10] An effort was made by all participants to make sure they would be seen and remembered. Lyman Brewster later referred to these as "alibi" dances.

Meanwhile the Northern Cheyennes had been making good use of the dead sheep. They mobilized thirty-three wagons to haul off the carcasses. Daut told the Cheyennes to skin the sheep, give him the hides, and they could have the carcasses for meat. The Cheyennes spent the next three days hauling wagonload after wagonload back to the reservation at Ashland and Indian Birney.[11] Joe Brown, Jr. of the Three Circle recalled that the smell of dead sheep permeated the Tongue River Valley all spring.[12] However, the Cheyennes also remember that winter as being the one winter when they were well fed.

For nearly seventy-four years the secret of who participated in the Bear Creek Raid was tightly held. Despite rewards for as much as $19,000 in today's dollars, no $40-per-month cowboy ever talked, even when drunk. While people speculated in hushed tones, $15,000 in damage money was deposited anonymously in Selway's bank account to pay for the sheep. Selway refused the money and continued to pursue John B. Kendrick, whom he believed responsible, until the whole incident was largely forgotten. Kendrick continued to build his ranching fortune, became governor of the state of Wyoming, and served in the U.S. Senate until his death in 1933.

---

10 Interview and correspondence with Neil Thex.
11 Beach, *Faded Hoof Prints—Bygone Dreams*, John Daut's Story.
12 Joe Brown, Jr. conversation with Forest Dunning, 1960s.

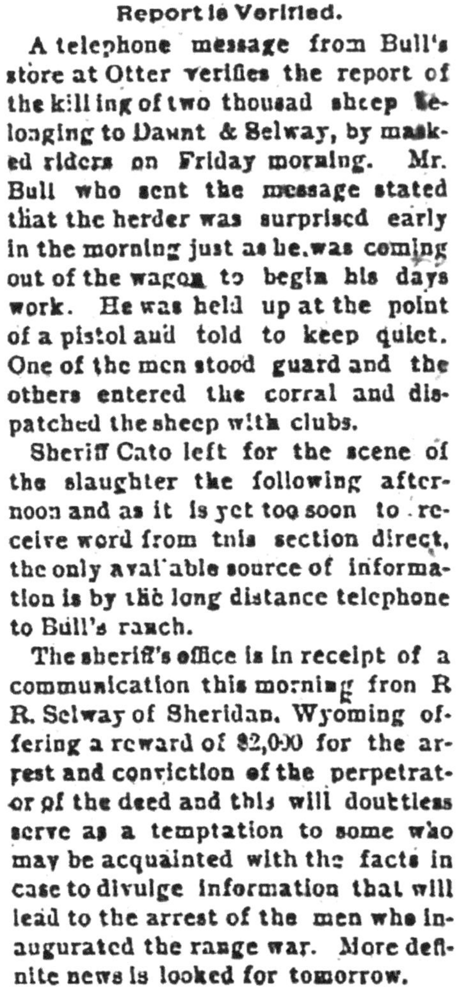

Report is Verified.

A telephone message from Bull's store at Otter verifies the report of the killing of two thousand sheep belonging to Dawnt & Selway, by masked riders on Friday morning. Mr. Bull who sent the message stated that the herder was surprised early in the morning just as he was coming out of the wagon to begin his days work. He was held up at the point of a pistol and told to keep quiet. One of the men stood guard and the others entered the corral and dispatched the sheep with clubs.

Sheriff Cato left for the scene of the slaughter the following afternoon and as it is yet too soon to receive word from this section direct, the only available source of information is by the long distance telephone to Bull's ranch.

The sheriff's office is in receipt of a communication this morning from R R. Selway of Sheridan, Wyoming offering a reward of $2,000 for the arrest and conviction of the perpetrator of the deed and this will doubtless serve as a temptation to some who may be acquainted with the facts in case to divulge information that will lead to the arrest of the men who inaugurated the range war. More definite news is looked for tomorrow.

Figure 4: Forsyth Times, January 8, 1901.

CHAPTER TWO

THE LYMAN BREWSTER TALE

The facts of the Bear Creek Sheep Raid were shrouded in mystery for the next seventy-four years. The incident was the subject of gossip, speculation, and misinformation until some details were finally reported in the Winter 1974 issue of *Montana: The Magazine of Western History* with a brief four-page article authored by Lyman Brewster. In his article, "December 1900: The Quiet Slaughter," Brewster reports that his father, George Brewster of the Quarter Circle U Ranch, and John B. Kendrick of the OW Ranch were leaders of the raid. Brewster also said his mother confirmed his father's participation after his death. Furthermore, he was told by J. H. "Shorty" Caddel, the last living participant and former employee of the Quarter Circle U, about the details of the raid during an automobile trip in 1955. This was followed by additional conversations and correspondence. Lyman Brewster waited until well after the deaths of all participants before he disclosed the list of raid participants and their actions that day for the historical record.

In the article Brewster reports that eleven men were in the raiding party. Led by John B. Kendrick and George Brewster, they were accompanied by Charles Thex, Horton Boal, Frank "Booker" Lacy, William "Bill" Munson, Frank McKinney, Walt Snider, Mahlon "Tug" Wilson, "Barney" Hall, and J. H. "Shorty" Caddel. He further identifies Munson, McKinney, Wilson, and Snider as OW cowboys, with Hall and Caddel as riders for the Quarter Circle U. Boal, Thex, and Lacy were fellow ranch owners in the area. Brewster briefly describes the conditions that led to the raid, the use of "alibi" dances to cover up the men's participation, and the importance of "range orders" to the cattle community. He particularly emphasizes that no humans were killed or injured and that the "conspiracy of silence" kept the raid's secrets for seventy-four years. "December 1900: The Quiet Slaughter" is a particularly apt description of the raid.

There are a few problems with the article. Brewster claims that Barney Hall and Shorty Caddel were Quarter Circle U cowboys at the time of the raid. In fact, neither man was an employee of the Quarter Circle U at the time. The 1900 census does not show them as residents of the Quarter Circle U either.[1] Shorty Caddel did work for the Quarter Circle U in subsequent years and Lyman Brewster knew him well. However, court records show Caddel to be in the employ of Horton Boal of the Three X Bar Ranch[2] at the time of the raid, not the Quarter Circle U.

Perhaps a "Barney Hall" may have worked at the Quarter Circle U at some point after the event but not at the time of the raid. "Barney" Hall is probably Barna Hall, a cousin of Levi Howes and owner of a ranch on Bear Creek, very near the location of the raid. Hall appears on the 1900 census records as a stockman on Bear Creek.[3] He was also the rancher most directly affected by the Selway sheep. These points speak overwhelming that Barna Hall was most likely the "Barney" Hall reported by Brewster. Barna Hall sold his ranch on Bear Creek in 1908 and went back to Massachusetts.[4] Lyman Brewster could not have known him well because Lyman was born in 1903 and would have been only five years old when Hall left.

---

[1] 1900 Federal Census Records of School District 01, Custer County, Montana.
[2] Probate documents of Horton Boal, Rosebud County, Montana.
[3] 1900 Federal Census Records of School District 01, Custer County, Montana.
[4] *Echoing Footsteps*, Barna Hall Family.

Figure 5: Lyman Brewster, author of "December 1900: The Quiet Slaughter."

Brewster speculates that the sheep were clubbed from horse-back since most cowboys abhorred work on the ground. While that may have been the plan, the time line does not support that contention. The raiders arrived at daylight on the morning of December 28 and completed their work before dark, a duration of ten hours. That the men randomly rode into 2,200 sheep swinging clubs until all had been killed strains credibility. To deliver a killing blow to a yearling ewe requires an accurate strike to the forehead with sufficient force to crush the bone into the frontal lobe of the brain. Swinging a club from a moving horse at a moving sheep is not conducive to accuracy. Some would be stunned rather than killed, others injured by plunging horses, and keeping the herd together would be problematic. Horses trying to maneuver around dead and injured sheep frantically trying to get away plus the smell of blood would panic even the gentlest of horses. To kill that many sheep in eight to ten hours of daylight requires at a minimum one dead sheep every thirty seconds. It is more likely that an organized and systematic method was used.

While the Brewster article may not be 100 percent accurate, Brewster does provide the essential facts on which to begin an accurate examination of the event. When supplemented by other facts gleaned from subsequent interviews with John Daut, the Selway family, Charles Thex, Frank Lacy, Levi Howes, Leota Kimes Dunning, Maime "Peachy" Cox, and other pioneers in the neighborhood, a clearer picture of the event and its historical context unfolds. Lyman Brewster is to be celebrated for his courage and sense of history with the contribution of his article.

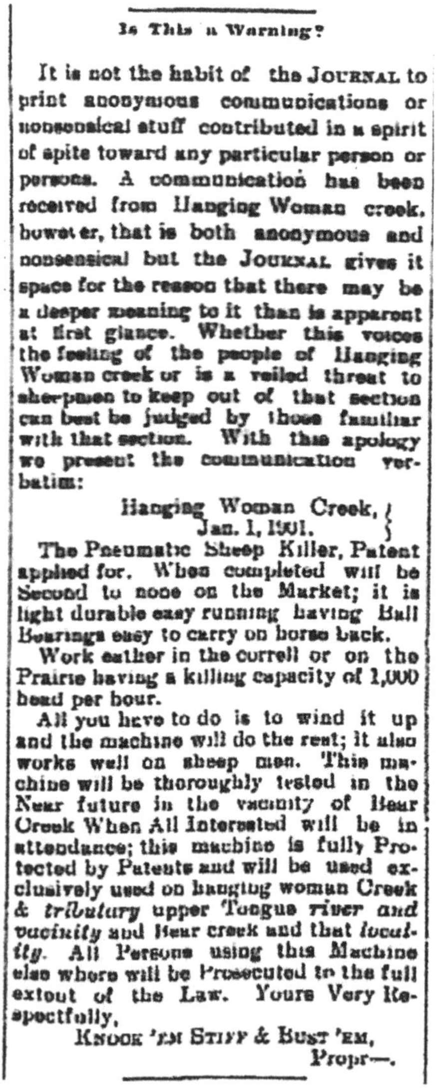

Is This a Warning?

It is not the habit of the JOURNAL to print anonymous communications or nonsensical stuff contributed in a spirit of spite toward any particular person or persons. A communication has been received from Hanging Woman creek, however, that is both anonymous and nonsensical but the JOURNAL gives it space for the reason that there may be a deeper meaning to it than is apparent at first glance. Whether this voices the feeling of the people of Hanging Woman creek or is a veiled threat to sheepmen to keep out of that section can best be judged by those familiar with that section. With this apology we present the communication verbatim:

Hanging Woman Creek, Jan. 1, 1901.

The Pneumatic Sheep Killer, Patent applied for. When completed will be Second to none on the Market; it is light durable easy running having Ball Bearings easy to carry on horse back.

Work eather in the correll or on the Prairie having a killing capacity of 1,000 head per hour.

All you have to do is to wind it up and the machine will do the rest; it also works well on sheep men. This machine will be thoroughly tested in the Near future in the vicinity of Bear Creek When All Interested will be in attendance; this machine is fully Protected by Patents and will be used exclusively used on hanging woman Creek & tributary upper Tongue river and vacinity and Bear creek and that locality. All Persons using this Machine else where will be Prosecuted to the full extout of the Law. Yours Very Respectfully,

KNOCK 'EM STIFF & BUST 'EM, Propr—.

Figure 6: Yellowstone Journal, *January 17, 1901.*

CHAPTER THREE

THE INFORMATION CONUNDRUM

It is difficult to put flesh on the bones of the Brewster article because reliable sources are sorely lacking. Initial reports to Sheriff O. C. Cato came by way of a primitive telephone system at the Three Circle[1] and Bull Ranches[2] by excited ranchers who had only secondhand information. These reports were then picked up by newspapers scrambling for any details, which further compromised the facts. Early reports of sheep being "rimrocked" (stampeded over a cliff)[3] and killed by "giant powder" proved to be incorrect. Only after Sheriff Cato traveled over 100 miles from Miles City to Bear Creek and returned days later was accurate information available.

About the only information he learned, however, was that 2,113 sheep belonging to John Daut and R. R. Selway had been clubbed to death by persons unknown. He gathered up a few bloody clubs and returned to Miles City. By the time he returned, it was a story without much new information. Also, a remarkable "conspiracy of silence" descended on the area as residents closed ranks behind the cattlemen who had done the deed.

More information came much later, from a series of interviews

---

[1] Arthur Hayes, Jr. interview with Forest Dunning.
[2] Beach, *Faded Hoof Prints—Bygone Dreams*, John Daut's Story.
[3] *The Sheridan Post*, January 3, 1901.

done in the 1930s under the auspices of the Works Progress Administration to record the history of Powder River County. Maude Beach conducted a series of interviews with pioneers including John Daut, Levi Howes, Charles Thex, and relatives of R. R. "Bob" Selway. Daut and the Selways were very forthcoming, as injured parties are likely to be, while the "silence" continued on the cattlemen's side. Through the Daut interview, considerable valuable information was learned about the participation of John B. Kendrick and Levi Howes in the negotiations with Daut to leave the Bear Creek area before and after the raid. In 1989 the Powder River Historical Society published these interviews in a book titled *Faded Hoof Prints—Bygone Dreams.*

Another source was the series of interviews done between 1957 and 1962 by Bob Helvey. These were taped interviews of "old-timers," which were then transcribed. Informants included Frank "Booker" Lacy, J. H. "Shorty" Caddel, Levi Howes, Leota Kimes Dunning, and others. Unfortunately, there are several problems with these interviews. The informants were very elderly at the time of the interviews, in their late eighties and early nineties, so their memories are suspect. Also, they were reluctant to inform on friends and neighbors whose families were still in the area ("conspiracy of silence"). They had biases and prejudices that colored their memories. Lastly, the late 1950s and 1960s technology available for recording and transcription was poor, which left gaps and blanks in the transcripts.

The most productive and accurate information was obtained by tedious examination of public records such as census reports, abstract records, payroll records, court records, tax reports, and obituaries.

A final source were the family histories and genealogy publications of the local area. While their credibility at times may be suspect, they often provide context and information unavailable elsewhere. Books such as *Echoing Footsteps* (Powder River County) and *They Came and They Stayed* (Rosebud County) were vital sources to researchers of this incident.

Faded Hoof Prints --- Bygone Dreams

STORIES FROM MONTANA'S
GREATEST LIVESTOCK FRONTIER,
POWDER RIVER COUNTRY

compiled by
Maude L. Beach

edited by
Robert L. Thaden, Jr.

Figure 7: Cover of Faded Hoof Prints—Bygone Dreams, *courtesy of the Powder River Historical Society.*

While no one source was definitive, the combination of sources was instructive as to the probable course of events. The following chapters attempt to put the Bear Creek Raid in its proper historical context as well as inform the reader about the raid and its aftermath.

CHAPTER FOUR

THE BIG SKY
GETS SMALLER

Montana is the fourth-largest state in the nation after Alaska, California, and Texas. Located in the northwestern part of the United States, it stretches for about 560 miles from east to west and 320 miles north to south. To its north is Canada, where it shares the longest common border between the United States and any of the fifty states. Two of the largest rivers in the United States are separated by the Continental Divide and have their headwaters in Montana: the mighty Missouri, which flows east into the Mississippi, and the Columbia via the Snake, which flows west into the Pacific. It is the home of numerous mountain ranges mostly located in the western part of the state, while the eastern area is dominated by great sweeping plains cut by productive river valleys. In the eastern part of the state, the Missouri and Yellowstone Rivers dominate the territory with their associated tributaries. One of the unique features of the Yellowstone River is that its major tributaries flow north from Wyoming, rather than east, to their junctions with the Yellowstone. The Bighorn, Tongue, Rosebud, Powder, and Little Missouri Rivers all run north to drain the southeastern quadrant of Montana.

The Bear Creek Raid took place in southeastern Montana, very close to the Wyoming border, between two tributaries of the Tongue River—Otter Creek and Hanging Woman Creek. More

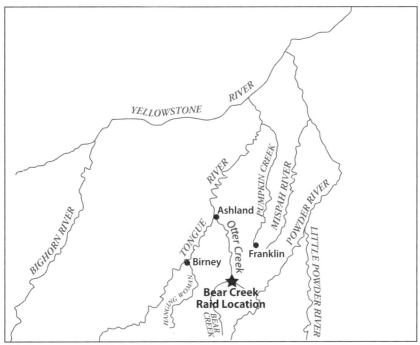

Figure 8: Southeastern Montana; the Bear Creek Raid location is marked with a star.

specifically, the site is located at the junction of Tooley Creek and Bear Creek shortly before Bear Creek joins Otter Creek.

Montana is unique among the western states in that it was settled from west to east rather than from east to west. When gold was discovered in Alder Gulch in 1863, the gold communities of Virginia City, Bannack, and Helena sprang up, and thousands of miners flowed into the western part of the state in the 1860s. Gold and silver was followed by the discovery of huge copper deposits in Butte, which led to rapid settlement in western Montana. Ranches and farms grew up near these communities to support the mining industry.

Most of eastern Montana was withheld from white settlement because it was Indian Territory, which included the Sioux, Northern Cheyenne, Northern Arapaho, Crow, Blackfeet, and smaller tribes. It wasn't until after the Battle of the Little Bighorn

Figure 9: Waiting For A Chinook *by Charles Russell (public domain).*

in 1876 that these tribes were defeated and settled on individual and much smaller reservations. With the virtual elimination of the buffalo and control of hostile tribes, white settlement began in southeastern Montana in 1878.

Large cow herds started to come up from Texas during the following years, giving rise to the decade of the huge cattle syndicates. Vast tracts of "free grass" on public land made cattle raising a very profitable opportunity. By the mid-1880s, most of this land had been "claimed by prior use" to the benefit of large ranchers, including huge syndicates financed by European and British investors. Overgrazing was rampant, and little provision for winter feed was made. The terrible winter of 1886–87 resulted in losses of up to 90 percent and broke nearly all of these "cattle kings," putting most of them into receivership. At the same time, rapid advancement of the railroads allowed homesteaders to pour into the area to homestead on public land and cheap railroad land. This wave of settlement signaled the end of the big cattle bonanza.

Figure 10: Pumpkin Creek Pool (L. A. Huffman), courtesy of the Montana Historical Society.

As the 1880s came to an end, the southeast quarter of the state of Montana was changing rapidly. The buffalo had been exterminated, the Indians vanquished and confined to reservations, the railroads built, and the syndicates of largely foreign cattle companies bankrupt. Their remaining cattle, improvements, and crews were now controlled by receiverships with court-appointed managers.

Into this breach stepped the former managers for the old syndicates. They had the technical knowledge, access to new capital, managerial talent, and iron will to bring new cattle ranches out of chaos. However, now the railroads were bringing in hordes of new settlers who were fanning out into the countryside to homestead government land. Thus began a race between the "new" cattle kings and the settlers for control of land.

Another unwelcome consequence of the collapse of the great foreign-owned cattle companies was the rise of organized gangs of horse thieves and cattle rustlers. Because the number of cattle had been greatly diminished by deaths in the winter of 1886–87, the men formerly employed by those companies no longer had jobs. Some of these men drifted into a life of crime to varying degrees. Large gangs such as the Wild Bunch and Teton Jackson's outfit operated horse stealing enterprises on a grand scale, moving thousands of horses from Canada to New Mexico and back.[1] They also stole cattle, though insignificant numbers compared to horses.

During this period, there evolved a distinction between a cattle thief and a rustler. The remaining cattle following the 1886–87 winter were scattered far and wide, often drifting far from their home ranges. Many calves were not branded until the ownership of the defunct cattle companies was sorted out. Thousands of these calves grew to adulthood without brands, and ownership could not be proven. Many cowboys homesteaded, bought a few cows, and then put their own brand on these unbranded adult cattle, which were called "mavericks."

The term "rustler" originally referred to a man who aggressively pursued these unbranded cattle to increase his herd. In fact, the "new" cattle kings often paid their cowboys a bonus of two to five dollars a head to brand these mavericks for their ranches. However, as the 1880s ended, most of the true mavericks had been branded, and some of these rustlers began to put their brand on unbranded calves that could be separated from their branded mothers. Sometimes the calf's mother would be killed so the calf could be stolen. Thus, the terms "cattle thief" and "rustler" came to mean the same thing.

While the issue was not as bad in southeastern Montana as it was in Wyoming, the ownership of mavericks continued to vex the new cattle kings as they tried to gather the remaining cattle legally acquired from the bankrupt companies. The result was a period of violence in the early 1890s highlighted by the "Rustler's War" in Johnson County, Wyoming. This culture of violence permeated the entire region and served to exacerbate conflicts between residents of the open range in later years.

---

[1] Kelly, *The Outlaw Trail.*

Early in the decade of the 1890s, settlers filed their homesteads on land suitable for farming along flowing rivers and streams. As the decade progressed, land that could be easily irrigated dwindled. As early arrivers, the new cattlemen did all they could to retain the best land suitable for hay production. The winter of 1886–87 had taught cattlemen that access to a reliable winter supply of hay would be imperative for Montana ranching in the future. Therefore, they engaged in a major effort to tie up water sources for a secure hay supply and water for their livestock. Every member of a cattleman's family who became eligible to homestead on river or stream bottoms did so. They also financed their cowboys to file on land they wanted and bought those homesteads after they had "proved up."

Because of their access to capital, cattlemen also stood ready to buy out any homesteader who had "proved up" but "starved out." Another tactic was the purchase of "land script" to enhance their holdings. Land script was the right to purchase U.S. government land at a favorable price, usually $1.25 an acre. The right was given mostly to veterans in lieu of cash upon mustering out of the service. Since most of the script was freely transferable, much of it was sold by the original recipient for cash. Speculators accumulated the script and resold it to the highest bidder. The larger cattlemen were prime customers of these speculators.

Toward the end of the 1890s, most of the good farmland was taken, but settlers were still pouring into the area looking for their share of the American Dream. The importance of irrigation was proven by early arrivers, which resulted in nearly all land next to running water being homesteaded early. Now the only land available for homesteading or script purchase was located on marginally watered rangeland with springs and perennial streams. There was still plenty of U.S. government land, but it was only suitable for grazing livestock if it had access to water.

When a homesteader filed on a 160-acre parcel with a spring on it, they usually put up a perimeter fence, thereby rendering water unavailable to cattlemen grazing on adjacent public land. This led

Figure 11: Quarter Circle U Ranch in 1897, courtesy of the Montana Historical Society.

to problems between homesteaders and cattlemen when thirsty cattle pushed down fences, often with the assistance of a stout rope thrown by a cowboy. On the other hand, homesteaders rarely ate their own beef, opting instead for the cattle pushing their fences down. Homesteading on these marginal tracts was a gamble at best and a surefire loss at worst. The wisest cattlemen simply ignored the cattle butchering, bided their time, and bought out the land when the first dry year came and the homesteader starved out.

Another tactic frequently used by the larger cattlemen was the use of political power to withdraw U.S. government land from homesteading and then lease the land. This was done by supporting the transfer of timbered country to newly created U.S. Forest Reserves and then securing permits to graze these lands. Subsequent rules further cemented this "grazing right" by giving preference to current users of the forest land. Levi Howes of the Circle Bar Ranch and Captain Joe T. Brown of the Three Circle Ranch were two of the more successful cattlemen to use this technique in the Birney/Otter area.[2]

---

[2] Howes, *Montana Territory*.

Figure 12: Three Circle Ranch bunkhouse, courtesy of the Hayes Family.

George Brewster of the Quarter Circle U Ranch and Captain Joe T. Brown secured favorable leases on the Northern Cheyenne Indian Reservation lands when the reservation was expanded in 1900. Both men served as presidents of the Montana Stock Growers Association and state legislators shortly after the turn of the century.

Several years after the Bear Creek Raid, John B. Kendrick of the OW Ranch on Hanging Woman Creek served in the Wyoming legislature, and as governor and U.S. senator for the state of Wyoming while building his cattle empire. He frequently used his political power to secure preference on land sales and favorable leases on the Crow Indian Reservation.[3]

All these men were politically well connected. For example, Captain Brown actually served as a captain in Roosevelt's Rough Riders and knew the future president.

Although neither man served in the legislature, Captain Calvin Howes and Levi Howes of the Circle Bar were very active in Montana political circles. The Howes family was instrumental in

---

[3] King, *The Empire Builders.*

the establishment of the Otter Post Office and the Custer National Forest.[4] These men were high-energy folks with vision, intelligence, and education. They knew the country and its people from years of managing huge cattle operations across wide swaths of federal land. Howes, Brown, and Kendrick ran cattle from the Yellowstone River south to the Bighorn Mountains in Wyoming and east to the South Dakota state line. While fiercely protecting their own interests, they were careful not to violate the prevailing norms of the larger community.

Sheep men came into southeast Montana as early as 1879 when John Burgess brought a flock of sheep from California to Miles City and sold most of them to Fort Keogh. However, he kept the nucleus of a herd and started a sheep ranch a few miles from Miles City. Other flock masters followed and settled in the immediate vicinity of Miles City, where they could sell meat to Fort Keogh, but were not a significant force in the area until after the railroad had arrived in 1882.

Large-scale sheep raising in Custer County did not begin until John Lloyd Selway and Charles Daly settled on the Pumpkin Creek drainage in 1881.[5] The Selway family had brought in 800 ewes from Oregon to Beaverhead County in Montana as early as 1865 to feed the gold miners in the western part of the state. By 1881 their flocks had outgrown their range, and they were looking for unoccupied grass. John O. Selway sent one of his six sons, John Lloyd Selway, with a band of about 2,500 sheep to the Miles City area to scout out a new sheep ranch.[6] There Lloyd Selway met Charles Daly, who had acquired about 600 ewes and was also looking for unoccupied territory. The two men decided to form a loose partnership in which they would help each other and share expenses for shearing, freighting, and defense. Because there was no market for lambs until the railroad reached Miles City, the Selways kept their natural increase

---

[4] Howes, *Montana Territory.*
[5] Brown and Felton, *Before Barbed Wire.*
[6] Beach, *Faded Hoof Prints—Bygone Dreams,* Selway Family story.

and grew their herds. They were good operators, selling wool in the spring and lambs in the fall. Since the Pumpkin Creek area was unoccupied by cattlemen, the Selways ranged their flocks widely to establish "first use" of the country and thereby acquire a "range right" to discourage incoming cattlemen from settling near them.

"First in use, first in right" was informally but firmly recognized throughout the West regarding land and water. Land held by "squatters" was recognized as valid up to the time when the area was properly surveyed, at which time the squatter could file for his rights under the various Homestead Acts. Accurate survey data was a recurring problem in the West throughout the homestead era. Accurate locations of Indian reservations, railroad land, forest reserves, parks, and national monuments constantly conflicted with settlement land.

While water was ultimately determined by state constitutions to be property of the state, most western states determined the allocation and distribution of their water to be "first in use, first in right," thereby creating "water rights."

At the time, cattlemen believed that sheep and cattle could not occupy the same range because sheep grazed the grass too close to the ground and ruined water holes, and because their smell caused cattle to avoid areas used by sheep. While this was true when areas were overgrazed, it was later learned that under proper management the two industries could operate on the same range under the same owner.

When cattlemen tried to move into Pumpkin Creek areas that looked promising, a band of sheep would show up to encourage the cattlemen to move on to a different territory.[7] Ultimately sheep men and cattlemen negotiated rough limits to their ranges and tolerated each other. In later years these limits were delineated by plowing a "deadline" furrow to separate the two ranges. However, this was usually only the case when the sheep were first in the area and not the other way around.

---

[7] Brown and Felton, *Before Barbed Wire.*

Following the arrival of the railroad in 1882, the number of homesteaders and sheep operators increased sharply in south-eastern Montana. Sheep could be hauled into the area by rail rather than trailed the hundreds of miles previously required. Furthermore, a rail head meant that wool and castrated male lambs (wethers) could be moved back East for sale with relatively little time and expense. Many new homesteaders were farmers settling along flowing streams to raise grain, hay, and vegetables, and they provided a ready market for sheep men. The farmers fed newly weaned wether lambs to slaughter weight on the hay and small grains they raised. In this respect, the sheep men were ahead of the cattlemen in recognizing the benefit of feeding grain to slaughter.

In the early 1890s the cattlemen's business model was still mostly built on low-cost grass. Steers were kept until they were two to four years of age and marketed in the fall. Most of these grass-fattened cattle went directly to slaughter without the ben-efit of hay and grain. However, as the cheap grass and water was taken up by homesteaders, ranchers began to appreciate the value of shortening the marketing age of their beef. Thus the rise of the farmer/feeder began to demonstrate economic sense.

Early homesteaders quickly learned the value of irrigation in Montana and began raising alfalfa hay, oats, and barley. There was an excellent market from the large cattle and sheep outfits for high-protein hay to supplement their herds through tough win-ters. Stock growers could raise the same number of animals on fewer acres with winter feeding. However, as the 1890s came to a close, the good land along flowing rivers and streams was all taken. Newcomers who wanted homesteads now had to move onto more-marginal land without irrigation. They began to homestead springs and perennial streams, which were the lifeblood of the cattlemen and large sheep men grazing free grass.

The politicians quickly recognized that a family could not pros-per on the 160 acres originally allocated under the Homestead Act in these areas of Montana. Some adjustments were made to allow for larger homesteads of up to 640 acres under the Desert

Figure 13: Abandoned homestead near Otter, Montana.

Land Act. Since Montana rangeland could only support one cow on thirty to forty acres, even these larger homesteads could not support a family except in the wettest of years. The result was the "bust" of most homesteaders after a few years.

At the turn of the twentieth century, eastern Montana was almost all settled except for the land that was the most unproductive. Homesteading continued until the 1920s, but most Montana homesteads were starved out after a few years and acquired for very little money by resident stockmen. One discouraged homesteader nailed the following sign on his door:

FORTY MILES FROM WATER
FORTY MILES FROM WOOD
FORTY MILES FROM HELL
FOR ALL I KNOW
ME, I'M GONE FOR GOOD.[8]

---

[8] *Echoing Footsteps*, Powder River County Extension Homemakers Council.

CHAPTER FIVE

THE INVASION
OF OTTER CREEK

The Otter Creek and Tongue River valleys had been fully settled by 1900.[1] Very few parcels that bordered flowing water
were available for settlement. The communities of Birney, Ashland,
and Otter were fully established, each with a post office, general
store, school, and church.

Otter Creek was dominated by the Howes outfit (Circle Bar
Ranch) and Colonel Thomas Bryan's Bug Ranch, but the area had
been fully homesteaded for some years by smaller operators. Many
of the smaller operators were former cowboys from the big ranches
who were on good terms with the big outfits.

In the early 1880s, Captain Calvin Howes and his family
strategically homesteaded Otter Creek at the mouths of Taylor
Creek and Indian Creek. Later he acquired homesteads from his
former partners J. W. Strevell and John Miles. In addition, he used
his capital to buy out other homesteads as people left the area.
Other family relations including nephews Barna Hall and Freeman
Howes also took up homesteads in the vicinity. In 1898 Captain
Howes turned over active management to his son Levi Howes and
returned to Massachusetts.

Colonel Thomas Bryan used a similar strategy to grow the "Bug,"

---

[1] Howes, *Montana Territory.*

Figure 14: John B. Kendrick, courtesy of the Trail End State Historic Site (Manville Kendrick Collection).

but by 1900 age and ill health began to take its toll. Unable to personally manage his large holdings, he took in partners who had nearby homesteads including "Shorty" Badgett (not to be confused with Shorty Caddel), who became manager of the Bug Ranch. Colonel Bryan then retired to Miles City and California.

The Hanging Woman drainage was dominated by the outsized personality of John B. Kendrick of the OW Ranch. Kendrick became the manager of the Converse Cattle Company when it went broke after the winter of 1886–87. A hard-driving, extremely talented man, he went from a $30-a-month cowboy with little education to become a true "cattle king," owning or controlling hundreds of thousands of acres and thousands of cattle. He had come up the Texas Trail and fought Indians, rustlers, grasshoppers, and weather to build his empire. John B. Kendrick brooked no opposition to the "range orders" that he issued and was fully prepared to back up those orders with any means necessary.[2]

He hired cowboys to homestead strategic water resources and then bought those homesteads back from them. A prolific user of script to buy land, he had a script broker in Minneapolis on the lookout for any script that could be used in the OW area.[3] He tolerated homesteaders but let them know that he was ready to buy them out if they wanted to leave. Unsubstantiated oral history hints that if they were particularly irksome, they might be visited by Charlie Flory, his wolf killer, as a not so subtle warning to not butcher any OW cattle because he would be watching.

On the East Fork of Hanging Woman were Horton Boal, son-in-law of W. F. "Buffalo Bill" Cody, of the Three X Bar, and Frank "Booker" Lacy of the Campstool. Both of these smaller ranches claimed range directly adjacent to the site of the sheep killing.

The Upper Tongue River country in Montana (between Ashland and the Wyoming state line) was heavily homesteaded by 1900. Again, most of the flowing water along the Tongue River was taken and homesteaders were beginning to move up the side creeks. The two largest ranches remaining on the river were the Quarter Circle U Ranch owned by George Brewster and the Three Circle Ranch owned by Captain Joe T. Brown. Both ranchers had thousands of cattle ranging throughout the area. George Brewster was a particularly close ally with John B. Kendrick. In fact, Brewster met his wife-to-be at the OW when she was visiting Kendrick's wife.[4] The two families were close friends for many years.

This was the cast of characters into which R. R. "Bob" Selway stepped when he decided to try and expand his sheep range. Due

---

2 Brewster, "December 1900: The Quiet Slaughter."
3 King, *The Empire Builders.*
4 Brewster, "December 1900: The Quiet Slaughter."

to the recent departure of the "Old Bulls"—Captain Calvin Howes and Colonel Thomas Bryan—from active management, Selway may have perceived that the two largest ranches on Otter Creek were in a weakened condition when he decided to bring sheep into the Otter Creek drainage. While that statement may be speculative, there is no doubt about what Selway did.

R. R. Selway and his foreman, John Daut, formed a partnership in which Selway would provide the financing for two bands of sheep on the Otter Creek drainage. Daut provided on-the-ground management. The basis of the partnership was a sheep lease. Under normal lease terms, the owner provided the sheep, sheep wagon, and one year's supplies in exchange for half the lambs and half the wool. The lessee furnished all care, range management, shearing, feed, mineral expenses, and death loss above 5 percent. Above 5 percent the lessee made up the difference from his share of the lambs. This encouraged the lessee to operate in a workmanlike manner, and under normally favorable circumstances he could buy the band from the owner after two or three years.

The most sheep that could be managed by one man was about 2,500 ewes, which was called a band. At the time of the raid, Bob Selway had more than 100 bands "on shares" in addition to his own sheep on Pumpkin Creek.[5] Furthermore, Selway was prepared to back Daut in the establishment of a homestead on Tooley Creek, and using script filed on seventy-two tracts of forty acres each on strategic springs and streams in the Tooley/Bear Creek area. When Daut hired W. P. Flynn, a Miles City surveyor, to survey the seventy-two tracts, the word spread quickly that the cattlemen's range was under attack.

Daut first moved into the Otter Creek area in 1900 and applied for Desert Land entries on behalf of himself and his wife on an important spring at the upper end of Tooley Creek. He built a small house, root cellar, and a small set of corrals in preparation for bringing in the Selway sheep. There was little objection in the

---

5 Beach, *Faded Hoof Prints—Bygone Dreams*, Selway Family story.

beginning. Daut was just another homesteader exercising his legal right to file on public land. However, when the surveyor showed up on other tracts and disclosed that he was working for one of the largest sheep men in the state of Montana, concern swept the area.

The first confrontation, in November 1900, was a face-to-face warning to John Daut at his homestead not to bring in sheep. While W. P. Flynn and John Daut were surveying his homestead, they were visited by Levi Howes and three other cattlemen. Howes stated that he and the men with him were members of a "settlers' committee" consisting of seventeen landowners in the local area.[6] Their purpose for the visit was to oppose the introduction of sheep on public range in the Otter Creek area. When Daut pointed out to the cattlemen that he was just exercising his legal homestead rights and should be able to run his choice of livestock on his own place, Howes replied that Daut's homestead was not the problem, it was the introduction of Selway's sheep onto nearby public land that he considered "their territory."

The Tooley, Little Bear, and Big Bear Creeks area was important grazing land to local cattlemen. They used the area in late fall before moving their cattle to creek bottoms for the winter. Furthermore, they had fought fires on that land all summer[7] and did not intend to allow Daut and Selway to graze it off and starve their cattle. The meeting ended with the stern warning that if Daut and Selway brought sheep into the country there would be trouble. They reiterated that under the traditional "first in use, first in right" principle, this was closed range.

Daut thought he was legally right and felt that the cattlemen were bluffing. He continued with the surveys into the month of November. His wife was very concerned that "something bad might happen," but Daut reassured her that the cattlemen were bluffing and everything would turn out alright.

Early in November two bands of sheep totaling 8,500 head

---

6 Beach, *Faded Hoof Prints—Bygone Dreams*, John Daut's Story.
7 Joe Brown, Jr. conversations with Forest Dunning, 1964.

Figure 15: Sheep along the Powder River (L. A. Huffman), courtesy of the Montana Historical Society.

were slowly trailed into the Tooley/Bear Creek drainage. When they crossed the "deadline" furrow on the divide between Bradshaw and Taylor Creeks, the die was cast. The last camp before the final move was on Taylor Creek just above the Circle Bar. That camp was perceived as a slap in the face to the cattlemen. The sheep were then moved in two bands to Tooley Creek. The larger band was bedded at Daut's homestead and the smaller at the junction of Tooley and Bear Creeks under Dan Squires' care. The larger herd was later taken to a new camp on Bear Creek with two herders. Each day the sheep were moved by their herders from their bedding grounds and out to graze the public land claimed by the cattlemen.

Shortly after the sheep had arrived, several hundred head of thirsty horses with the Circle Bar brand were stampeded through the Tooley Creek flock, scattering and injuring several sheep.[8] Daut's wife was quite distraught following the event and begged her husband to leave the Otter Creek area. By this time Daut thought he was too deeply committed to be scared off. However, a few days later a similar stampede again scattered and killed several sheep at the Bear Creek camp.[9] In response, Daut added his camp tender, Ellis, to the two herders at Bear Creek and armed the camp.

The sheep bones from the November incident caused confusion in later years about the true location of the December 28 raid.[10] Many people did not know that the Cheyennes had hauled the carcasses from the December 28 raid site back to the reservation.

The next event was a written warning in early December nailed to the lower herd's sheep wagon. The warning read:

MOVE THESE SHEEP EAST OF BRADSHAW CREEK OR EVERY DAMN ONE OF THEM WILL BE KILLED. BY ORDER OF THE SETTLERS COMMITTEE. IF THIS DON'T MOVE OUT THESE SHEEP, WE WILL KILL THE PARTIES THAT BROUGHT THEM IN.

COMMITTEE[11]

Daut chose to ignore the warning.

On December 28, 1900, the Bear Creek Raid destroyed 2,113 head of Daut's sheep.

A few days after the raid, another warning was delivered telling Daut to move his remaining sheep or that band would also be destroyed. With a totally distraught wife, Daut left word with a post cutting crew that he would be willing to move. Two days later Daut was visited in person by John B. Kendrick, who noted that

---

8 Leota Kimes Dunning interview with Bob Helvey; additional information in Helvey interview with Shorty Cadell (via Helvey's undocumented conversation with Luther Dunning referenced in both interviews).

9 Ibid.

10 Interview with Dick Fletcher and interviews/correspondence with Neil Thex.

11 Beach, *Faded Hoof Prints—Bygone Dreams*, John Daut's Story.

so far there had been no humans hurt and he would like to keep it that way. He recognized that Daut and Selway had a legitimate damage claim for the loss of the sheep. Kendrick then presented a typewritten agreement, which required that Daut remove the sheep and leave the area for fifty years. Daut asked that he be compensated for his share of the sheep and the move be delayed until the following fall so he could find other land on which to relocate. That proviso was agreed to, and an additional $4,000 was raised by subscription to pay for his house and share of the dead sheep.[12] He was given until October 1, 1901, to move on.

From that point on Daut was not bothered in any way and relocated to the Powder River by the deadline.

The Committee had prevailed.

---

[12] Howes, *Montana Territory*.

THE COMMON DEFENSE
Otter Creek Defenders and
Company C Montana Militia

Throughout the West in general, and in this area in particular, white settlers often rallied together for their common defense. Two groups, the Otter Creek Defenders and Company C of the Montana State Militia, were organized prior to the raid and illustrate the community's interest in self-defense.

After the Northern Cheyenne Reservation was established in 1884, settlers in the vicinity began to informally organize self-defense forces to protect their families against feared Cheyenne "outbreaks."

When the reservation was created, the Northern Cheyennes were scattered on other reservations. Those with close relatives in the Sioux Tribe were mostly at the Pine Ridge Agency in South Dakota. Some were at Fort Keogh near Miles City, Montana, as prisoners of war and scouts for General Miles, and others were with the Southern Cheyennes at the Darlington Agency in Oklahoma. There was also a small number with the Northern Arapaho tribe on the Wind River Reservation in Wyoming. From 1884 to nearly 1900, Cheyenne families journeyed to the Tongue River Agency where the tribe was reunited. Because this influx of new arrivals was largely spontaneous and not approved by the Indian Department, there were not enough rations appropriated to feed everyone. This led to periods of starvation on the reservation and

Figure 16: Captain Joseph T. Brown, courtesy of the Hayes Family.

Figure 17: Otter Creek Defenders, circa 1896, courtesy of Neil Thex. Barna Hall is in the back row, 2nd to left. Clarence Wulfjen (John B. Kendrick's brother-in-law) is also in the back row, 2nd to right. Charlie Thex is in the back row on the far right. Levi Howes is in the 3rd row, 3rd to right. Gus Howes is 2nd to right in the same row.

occasional Cheyenne raids on neighboring settler's cattle. In at least three incidents, white settlers were killed when they rode up on Cheyennes butchering their beef.

The name "Otter Creek Defenders" grew out of a more formal militia organized by Levi Howes of the Circle Bar Ranch in response to a feared Northern Cheyenne outbreak in1897. The settlers along Otter Creek and their cowboys formed a militia following the murder of sheepherder Dan Hoover in 1897. Howes built a small rock "fort" on a conical hill above the Circle Bar headquarters in response to expected Indian trouble and led a "militia" force of men to Ashland, Montana, to confront the Cheyennes if necessary. Here they were joined by another force from the Upper Tongue River under the command of First Lieutenant Joe T. Brown and Second Lieutenant George Brewster, which later was designated "Company C" of the Montana State Militia. Although these organizations were never used against the Cheyennes, Company C was mobilized in 1898 to serve with the Rough Riders in the Spanish-American War with newly promoted Captain Joe T. Brown commanding.

When the serenity of the Otter Creek, Hanging Woman, and Birney communities were threatened by an invasion of sheep, it is highly likely that the Otter Creek Defenders militia was called up by Levi Howes to oppose the sheep invaders.

One can only speculate on the membership of the Committee, which planned and executed the Bear Creek Raid. The eleven participants of the raid reportedly were ranch owners John B. Kendrick, George Brewster, Charlie Thex, Horton Boal, and "Booker" T. Lacy, and trusted cowboys Bill Munson, Frank McKinney, "Tug" Wilson, Walt Snider, "Barney" Hall, and J. H. "Shorty" Caddel.

The organization of the Otter Creek Defenders may have been reorganized to oppose sheep as the Committee without Captain Brown but with George Brewster and John B. Kendrick. Seen in the picture of the Otter Creek Defenders are Levi Howes, Augustus Howes, Freeman Howes, Charles Thex, Clarence Wulfjen (John B. Kendrick's brother-in-law), Dan Kelty, and Charlie Field. It would not be a far reach to say that some of the landowners in the Otter Creek area who were members of the Otter Creek Defenders were probably also members of Levi Howes' Committee four years later.

CHAPTER SEVEN

DONNING THE MASKS
The Cattlemen

When R. R. Selway began his "invasion," he should have known the tenor of the communities he was about to enter. While the leaders of the participants were John B. Kendrick and George Brewster, they were just a small part of a larger community dependent on the cattle industry. Many of the local homesteaders were former employees of the big ranches and acted as their part-time help. Others sold hay, grain, lumber, and other goods and services to the large outfits. There was very little of the "big versus little" animus like that found in Johnson County, Wyoming. The big ranches treated their employees and neighbors as friends. Everyone knew everyone else and were in every sense a community. If something threatened the community, everyone would rise to defend it. Therefore, when word spread that the area's main industry was threatened by a "sheep king," the larger community closed ranks to defend their friends.

Everyone looked to see how Kendrick, Howes, Brewster, Brown, and Badgett would react and provide the leadership to oppose a powerful and wealthy interloper. While Howes and Kendrick were most directly affected by the invasion, they could also count on the support of the nearly totally united Birney and Otter communities. However, it can be assumed that in the actual raid planning, only a very small circle of leaders was involved.

No one on Otter Creek would act without the active approval and support of Levi Howes (Circle Bar Ranch) and probably Shorty Badgett (Bug Ranch). Since Levi Howes disclosed in his first warning that there were seventeen members of the "settlers' committee," it can be assumed that there were at least twelve members who did not actively participate in the final raid but supported the action in other ways. Probably these members were other settlers on Otter Creek and a few from Hanging Woman. As these cattlemen were most directly impacted by Daut's entry on the Otter Creek range, they would be the most obvious suspects. It is likely they acted in a planning and support capacity to avoid recognition by Daut and his men.

There was another group of men who may have also been on the Committee. Five men came to Otter Creek from Wyoming in 1892, near the end of the Johnson County War. These men were "Shorty" Badgett, Joe Moore, "Kid" Anderson, Harvey Trusler, and Lee Tucker. Badgett, Anderson, and Trusler were reportedly partners in a horse ranch with Nate Champion, the leader of the small cattlemen at odds with the Wyoming Stock Growers Association. Lee Tucker and Joe Moore traveled with Kid Anderson and his mother, so it was likely that all five knew each other in Wyoming.[1]

Champion was killed at the KC Ranch by the Wyoming Stock Growers Association's hired army. The Johnson County "Invaders" had a "kill list" of about seventy-five men considered "rustlers" by the Wyoming Stock Growers. The "Invaders" were arrested by the U.S. Army after being surrounded by angry small cattlemen and townspeople at the TA Ranch.

These five tough cowboys all homesteaded on Otter Creek, married, raised families, and became respected stockmen. By 1900 they were well-established cattlemen who could be counted on to oppose a "sheep invader," by force if need be. The presence of Shorty Badgett of the Bug Ranch in this group indicates that at

---

[1] *Echoing Footsteps*, Trusler, Anderson, Moore (Shy), Tucker, and Badgett Family histories.

least some of these tough, competent cowboys were members of the seventeen "Committee men."

It was not that Selway and Daut did not know the rules. Years before the "invasion," a single furrow had been plowed on the divide between Otter Creek and Pumpkin Creek. Sheep were supposed to stay north of the "deadline" and cattle south.[2]

The Committee was active prior to and following the raid. When Circle Bar horses were stampeded twice through Daut's sheep, it is likely that Committeemen ordered and executed the deed. The note nailed to Daut's sheep wagon was further evidence of their presence. In fact, part of the reason that most of the participants in the December 28 raid were from Hanging Woman was that many of the Otter Creek members likely could have been identified by Daut and his herders. There were no interruptions during the raid, even though it was at the junction of two highly active wagon roads and within a half mile of the main road up and down Otter Creek, which indicates that Committee members were steering potential witnesses away from the area.

Of the remaining ranchers and cowboys who were participants in the raid, all shared close relationships with the Circle Bar or the OW.

Charlie Thex, while a cattle owner in his own right, had a long relationship with the Circle Bar and could have well represented Howes' interest as well as his own. Horton Boal of the Three X Bar was also directly impacted by Daut's sheep. His ranch was just "over the hill" on the East Fork of Hanging Woman Creek. In addition to his direct interest, the location of his ranch provided a prime departure point for the raid. His employee, J. H. "Shorty" Caddel, provided "muscle" to the cause. Booker Lacy was a former Kendrick employee and had a relationship with the OW similar to Thex with the Circle Bar. Walt Snider had a homestead about halfway between Daut's homestead and the OW and worked for

---

[2] Oral history confirmed by recollection of Marcus Stevens in a July 2018 interview. Stevens is the grandson of Levi Howes.

Early day Otter Creek Cowmen. Top row, L. to R.—Levi Howes, Sam Davidson (the cook), Unknown, Circle Bar hand. 2nd row down, Barna Hall, George (OW hand), Jim Shy, Gus Howes. 3rd row down, Chippy Caloraw, Booker Lacey. Front row, Ves Newell, Chas. Miller.

Figure 18: Otter Creek cattlemen, from Echoing Footsteps.

Kendrick. Bill Munson also had a homestead in Kendrick country and ran a few cows. Most of these cowboys were all loyal, long-time employees, many with supervisory positions. Bill Munson was wagon boss of the OW, Frank McKinney an OW foreman, and "Tug" Wilson a future OW wagon boss who stayed on the ranch until he died of old age.[3]

The final participant was Barna (Barney?) Hall. As a close relative of Levi Howes, he could well have been the representative of the Circle Bar. He had a direct interest in that he ran several hundred head of cattle and had his homestead on the Bear Creek drainage. As the nephew of Levi Howes' mother, he was a member of the Howes family. However, because he was a relatively late arrival to the area, he was much less recognizable than other members of the Howes family. John B. Kendrick may have also demanded

---

3 King, *The Empire Builders.*

a Howes family member be a participant to ensure that they had "skin in the game." In one unsupported report, Kendrick had previously been spurned by Levi Howes in a Kendrick-organized punitive expedition to rescue Wyoming cattlemen trapped at the TA Ranch in 1892 during the Johnson County War.[4] It is possible that he did not fully trust Levi Howes in a direct-action operation without family involvement. Except for Charlie Thex, all the raiders would have been from the Hanging Woman side of the hill without Barna Hall.

Lastly, there were the New Year's festivities. Nat Humphries of the 4D Ranch probably knew the raid date when he organized the Birney "alibi" dance that New Year's, and likewise other actors at the OW who planned the dance there. Someone had to give instructions as to when dances were to be scheduled and record who was invited for attendance. The coincidences suggest the presence of an organized and widespread support group in advance of the raid.

---

[4] Unpublished excerpt of Rosa Kendrick's diary labeled "Stories from My Father."

CHAPTER EIGHT

THE SHEEP KING "INVADERS"

W ho were these sheep men who tried to push their way into the Otter Creek drainage and why? To answer this question we must look into the background and character of Robert R. "Bob" Selway and John Daut.

At the time of the Bear Creek Raid, John Daut was a partner with Bob Selway with 8,500 head of sheep by means of a "sheep lease," as previously described. However, in Selway's other "share herds," the lessee found his own pasture on open range and took the risk of dealing with objecting cattlemen. This time, Selway seemed to have suspected that his entry would be opposed and made provisions for that opposition. Normally, leases were to one man with one band. In this case, there were two bands with five men. In addition to John Daut and his wife, there was a camp tender named E. E. Ennis and three herders—Dan Squires, a man named Newman, and another named Brown. According to some cattlemen, these men were a cut above the usual herders and looked to be more fighters than herders.[1] However, the presence of Daut's wife and the inaction of the herders during the stampedes that preceded the raid would argue against this charge.

---

[1] Howes, *Montana Territory*.

Figure 19: John Daut.

Selway also took the unusual step of filing on the springs and streams on tracts of forty acres each in his own name using script.[2] The Otter Creek and Hanging Woman Creek locations totaled 2,800 acres, so the net effect was to give him control of an additional 50,000-plus acres of public land through ownership of the water. It is clear that Daut was not just an itinerant sheepherder but a "stalking horse" for Bob Selway.

John Daut was born in Philadelphia to a recently immigrated German family. His father had a bakery shop and then a butcher shop before moving to a farm in Bloomfield, Pennsylvania, where John was raised with five brothers and sisters. Under his father's tutelage, young John learned the livestock business, especially raising sheep. Like many young men, when he was old enough he moved west to seek his fortune.

---

[2] Beach, *Faded Hoof Prints—Bygone Dreams*, John Daut and Selway Family recollections.

Daut sought out sheep outfits on his way west and earned his keep herding and shearing until he had saved enough money to start his own business. He owned a livery stable for a time in Crawford, Nebraska, and a butcher shop in Harrison, Nebraska. When the Panic of 1893 hit the country, he lost that business and moved farther west seeking employment in the sheep industry. He landed in Clearmont, Wyoming, and a job with Barney Brothers, a large sheep outfit. This led to his employ as a foreman with Charles Barney and experience with sheep operations on a large scale. He oversaw camp tenders and supplied numerous sheep camps in the Buffalo/Clearmont area. Here he encountered Bob Selway, who hired him to take over his Pumpkin Creek operations.

With Daut serving as foreman, Selway expanded his Pumpkin Creek operations over the next few years from 20,000 head to 62,000 head. He provided Daut a nice salary and a modern house for his wife. Impressed with Daut's ability to handle sheep and men, Selway selected Daut to partner with him in the occupation of a new sheep ranch in the Otter Creek area.

Daut figured that with Selway's backing and the excellent range in the Bear Creek/Tooley Creek drainage, he could do very well and end up with a sizable herd of his own. He gambled that legal systems in Montana had progressed to the point that "deadlines" and "range orders" would be replaced by sheriffs, county attorneys, judges, and juries. His thinking was premature.

Following the December 28 raid, Daut's partnership with Selway broke up.[3] Although Selway offered to fully replace the dead sheep at his expense if Daut would stay, Daut's wife was so traumatized by the event that he had to choose between Selway and his wife. With the $4,000 offered by Kendrick and Howes, Daut found land at the conjunction of the Little and Big Powder Rivers. In September 1901 he moved the remainder of his sheep to the new location and started again. However, bad luck continued

---

[3] Beach, *Faded Hoof Prints—Bygone Dreams*, John Daut's Story.

to plague him. In later years the Powder River flooded him out and after that he lost most of his flock to disease. He sold out his land and sheep in 1919 and ultimately worked for other ranches up and down the Powder River. Eventually he died in a mental institution.[4]

R. R. "Bob" Selway was the son of the early Montana pioneer, John O. Selway, and the brother of Lloyd Selway, who established the Selway Ranch on Pumpkin Creek in 1881. While Lloyd Selway had prospered moderately well, the winter of 1886–87 left the Selway Ranch decimated with thousands of dead sheep and $40,000 in debt. Young Bob Selway, then away at college, was asked to return and help right the ship. He was young, industrious, and nearly fearless. Taking charge with a vengeance, he quickly rebuilt the Selway Ranch, restored the flocks, added reservoirs, and irrigated alfalfa hayfields. He quickly recognized that control of water was the key to controlling public land. He became an expert in homestead law and script land law, and using that expertise expanded the Pumpkin Creek holdings to their maximum holding capacity.

By the late 1890s, Bob Selway had maxed out his range on Pumpkin Creek and began expanding his operations using sheep leases. He found reputable sheep men who had been herders and offered them the opportunity to own their own flocks. With a liberal sheep lease, he ran sheep with these men "on shares" if they could find the range to graze. Selway provided the sheep, a wagon, and supplies for a year in exchange for half the wool and half the lambs. Since there was still considerable open range not claimed by cattlemen, he found many takers. After two or three years, these "share" herds could be purchased from Selway at a good profit for both.

Selway was also instrumental in the organization of the Eastern Montana Wool Growers Association. This association was established to protect and enhance the business of sheep raising in eastern Montana. It was probably formed because the Montana Stock Growers Association was largely dominated by cattle interests,

---

[4] John Daut biography submitted to the Range Riders Museum, author unknown.

Figure 20: Robert R. Selway.

and sheep men felt their interests were not being protected. Many sheep men were members of both organizations and shared with cattlemen similar views on a variety of subjects. However, sheep men tended to take a more legalistic view of public land use than the cattlemen's "first in use, first in right" principal, which had dominated Montana politics since the beginning of the territory. Because they generally came later than cattlemen, their economic interest was served by challenging the old "range orders" that governed the demarcation between cattle range and sheep range. This led to the perception by cattlemen that sheep men were "Johnnie-come-lately moochers" out to take their livelihoods. However, as the country filled up and land was surveyed, legality began to outweigh custom in land-use conflicts.

As Selway grew in wealth and influence, he married and moved to a large home in Sheridan, Wyoming, where "cattle king" John B. Kendrick also now resided. While it is unknown if Selway was envious of Kendrick, something possessed him to challenge Kendrick when he decided to make the move into the Otter Creek country. He expressed the desire to have sheep operations closer to his home in Sheridan, but that could have been accomplished almost as well by moving to open land on the Powder River. A degree of arrogance may have convinced him that the country had progressed to the point that land law would supersede the "range orders" that the Committee had issued.

He chose unwisely.

CHAPTER NINE

THE LEADERS UNMASKED

Three men stand out as leaders of the Bear Creek Raid in the persons of John B. Kendrick, George Brewster, and Levi Howes.

JOHN B. KENDRICK

Figure 21: John B. Kendrick in 1900, courtesy of the Trail End State Historic Site (Hoff Collection).

John B. Kendrick was born on September 6, 1857, in Cherokee County, Texas. He was orphaned at an early age and raised by his half-sister and her husband. He only received a fifth-grade education before leaving home at the age of fifteen to become a cowboy breaking horses for his room and board. When the opportunity arose to join a 3,000-head cattle herd traveling from Matagora, Texas, to Wyoming, he jumped at the chance.[1] Paid $30 a month by the Snyder-Wulfjen Brothers of Round Rock, Texas, John B. did not blow his paycheck for liquor and women like his fellow cowboys. Instead he bought books and saved his money to buy cattle.

The herd arrived in the Lusk, Wyoming, area in August 1879, where Charles Wulfjen established his ranch, the ULA, named after his daughter Eula. Kendrick worked on this ranch for four and a half years, rising to the position of foreman. He was still saving his money and buying a few cows that Wulfjen let him run.

In 1883 Wulfjen and Kendrick returned to Texas where they put together another herd of 3,000 head to trail to Wyoming. Kendrick put his savings into these cheap cattle and then supervised the movement of this herd back to the head of the Cheyenne River in Wyoming. Three years later, in the fall of 1886, Wulfjen and Kendrick sold the ULA Ranch's range rights and cattle to the Converse Cattle Company. Kendrick's personal share by that time numbered 860 head. The Converse Cattle Company branded their cows the OW, and Kendrick became the superintendent of their cattle operations.

The timing of the Wulfjen/Kendrick sale to Converse was beyond fortunate, just three months before the horrific winter of 1886–87. However, Kendrick had noted that the whole country was overgrazed and already recognized that a tough winter could be problematic.[2] The losses to the Converse Cattle Company following that winter were close to 90 percent and put the company into insolvency. John B. Kendrick convinced the receivership judge

---

[1] Goergen, *One Cowboy's Dream.*
[2] King, *The Empire Builders.*

Figure 22: OW Ranch in 1900, courtesy of the Trail End State Historic Site (Hoff Collection).

to make him managing superintendent with full authority to run the affairs of the corporation on behalf of the court.

Kendrick found himself in the catbird seat. No one knew how many cattle were left alive as he went about the business of recovering the assets of the corporation. While it cannot be proved otherwise, it is widely suspected that Kendrick overstated the initial losses to the judge supervising the bankrupt Converse Cattle Company, and then used his own cash to purchase prime assets from the corporation at extremely favorable prices. He had on-the-ground control while the judge and owners were far away in Chicago, Minneapolis, Omaha, and Denver. Most of the other large cattle companies were in the same shape, and forced sales were everywhere. Due to the low initial valuation, Kendrick could show a profit to the judge for the first year of receivership, which ensured his continued management of the bankrupt corporation.

With total control of thousands of acres of land and cash from his partner Charles Wulfjen, Kendrick could show some positive return to the company while building up thousands of personal cattle on public land formerly under Converse control. Expenses were charged to the corporation, which accrued to the benefit of his personal cattle. Under this arrangement, tremendous amounts of cash were generated to the benefit of the Wulfjen/Kendrick partnership. In 1891 Kendrick married Eula Wulfjen, daughter of Charles Wulfjen, and the partnership was all in the same family. In 1897 Kendrick was able to buy the remnants of the Converse Cattle Company out of receivership for the insignificant sum of $38,436.

A farsighted man, in 1889 Kendrick moved the Converse Cattle Company to the OW Ranch in Montana where there was less competition for the public range. He also had noted there was more access to irrigated hay land along the Powder River. This flowing river was one of the last in the country to fill with homesteaders due to its poor water quality. Kendrick began to buy land on the Powder River, Hanging Woman Creek, and other water-rich areas with script, homesteading cowboys, and purchase of starved-out homesteaders.

By 1900 John B. Kendrick had fully consolidated his holdings in the Hanging Woman/Powder River area. He was running thousands of cattle there and was expanding his empire into northern Wyoming. He had extensive real estate holdings within the city of Sheridan, was a major stockholder and director of the First National Bank of Sheridan, and was beginning to dabble in coal mining in the Acme, Wyoming, area.[3] He was the "bull-of-the-woods" in the southern Montana/northern Wyoming country and had for over twenty years issued "range orders" and enforced them by any means necessary.[4] At the same time, he was sensitive to the changing times and sought to keep public opinion on his side. However, it is possible that he viewed Selway's attempted incursion into the Otter Creek/Hanging Woman range as a personal affront.

---

[3] King, *The Empire Builders.*
[4] Brewster, "December 1900: The Quiet Slaughter."

Following the December 28 raid, John B. Kendrick continued to build his empire and later entered the world of politics. In 1910 he won a seat in the Wyoming legislature. Shortly thereafter, he was elected governor for one term, and then served as U.S. senator for the state of Wyoming until his death in 1933. It is important to note that Kendrick was not a governor or U.S. senator until many years after the Bear Creek Raid.

GEORGE W. BREWSTER

Figure 23: George W. Brewster.

George Brewster was born on December 18, 1856, in Boston, Massachusetts. The descendent of Mayflower member William Brewster, he was as close to a "blue blood" as could be had at that time. Educated at Partridge Academy in Duxbury, Massachusetts, he found the East stifling and longed for the excitement of the West. His first stop was in Virginia City, Nevada, where his sister was teaching school. He found work in a quartz mill and learned the mining business until an injury caused him to move on. He traveled to the West Coast before deciding to try his luck in Butte, Montana, where the copper mines were going full blast. After spending some time in Butte, he soon tired of the mining scene.

Hearing that there were still buffalo in the southeastern part of the state, he decided he would like to hunt some before they were all gone. In 1882 he traveled to Miles City where he acquired a team, wagon, saddle horse, and camp outfit and started up the Tongue River. About three miles south of the junction of Hanging Woman Creek and the Tongue River, he found a nice big bend in the river with plenty of grass and water. Here he made a camp and set out to hunt buffalo. He liked the location so much that he took a squatter's right to a homestead until surveyors arrived a few years later, when he started the Quarter Circle U Ranch.[5] He acquired some cattle, and by 1884 had built a decent-sized herd.

Also that year, however, the Northern Cheyenne Reservation was established. Cheyenne Indians who had been prisoners of war at Fort Keogh, those who lived on the Darlington Agency in Oklahoma, and some who had been married into the Sioux Tribe in South Dakota began to populate the new reservation. In addition, under the Dawes Act, Indians were permitted to file homesteads. Several Cheyenne families with the help of the Catholic Church settled on both sides of Tongue River between the mouths of Otter Creek and Hanging Woman and up Hanging Woman Creek. The rations for these Cheyennes were not sufficient, so they had to supplement their government rations by hunting. Most of the time they hunted deer, antelope, and small game, but they occasionally killed cows owned by white ranchers. As the reservation proper became hunted out, the cattle killing became more and more problematic.

George Brewster took two significant actions to curb the Cheyenne predation of his cattle. First, he held a great feast at the Quarter Circle U where he invited all the nearby Cheyennes. During the feast several horse races, hoop games, and give-a-ways were conducted. A final contest of long-range marksmanship featured George Brewster perforating pie plates at 300 yards. He then

---

[5] *They Came and They Stayed*, Rosebud County History.

made a speech in which he asked the Cheyennes not to kill his cattle and pointed out his cattle could be recognized by the Quarter Circle U brand. The Cheyennes got the point, and thereafter he rarely lost his cattle to the hungry Cheyennes.

Later, when starvation on the reservation got particularly acute, he teamed up with Joe T. Brown, a Virginia Military Academy graduate, of the neighboring Three Circle Ranch to form Company C of the Montana State Militia of volunteers to protect settlers. Brown was the first lieutenant and Brewster the second lieutenant of this volunteer force. The State of Montana provided rifles and ammunition, but the men were not paid and provided their own horses. The unit deployed in the fall of 1890 after the murder of Hugh Boyle, a white boy killed by Cheyennes when they were caught with a butchered milk cow north of Lame Deer. After a "suicide by soldier" incident in which the two guilty Cheyenne youths were killed by the U.S. First Calvary, the Cheyennes were relatively peaceful for a few years.

In 1897 Company C was mobilized again when Don Hoover, a sheepherder, was killed by a group of four Cheyennes on the Tongue River, north of Ashland. They were joined at Ashland by the Otter Creek Defenders but disbanded after the four Cheyennes involved were sent to Miles City for trial.

George Brewster continued to build his ranch and cattle herd throughout the 1890s. In 1896 George met Grace Sanborn, a childhood friend of Eula Kendrick, at John B. Kendrick's OW Ranch, and they were married within a year. They had three children, Warren (b. 1898), Lyman (b. 1903), and Burton (b. 1906) and remained close friends of the Kendrick family for many years. It is not at all surprising that if John B. Kendrick asked George Brewster to help him deal with the Selway invasion, he would find a willing helpmate and co-organizer.

After the Bear Creek Raid, George Brewster became active in Montana state politics; he served three terms in the Montana legislature and was president of the Montana Stock Growers Association at the time of his sudden death in 1912.

LEVI HOWES

Figure 24: Levi Howes, courtesy of the Range Riders Museum.

As was reported in a previous chapter, Levi Howes was the middle son of Captain Calvin Howes, a former ship's captain. All three of the sons were born in Massachusetts while Captain Howes was aboard ship. In 1879 Captain Howes sold his ship and in early 1880 embarked with his family to Montana Territory to start in the cattle business. He and his family boarded the riverboat *Bachelor* at Bismarck, North Dakota, on the Missouri River "spring rise" in the spring of 1880. They elected to go to Miles City in Montana after talking to army officers who described the wonderful range country in that area.

Levi arrived in Miles City with his father at the age of twelve and initially stayed in Miles City with his mother and the rest of the family while his father built a ranch on the Tongue River, about fifty-five miles south of Miles City. The family moved to the new ranch once their house was built. His father purchased 160 head of local cattle and started to build his herd. At that time there were only five other ranches on the Tongue River. Over the next four years Captain Howes and his sons learned the cattle business from the ground up.

In 1882 Captain Howes entered a partnership with Judge J. W. Strevell and George Miles, a nephew of General Nelson Miles, to form the Circle Bar Ranch. With the additional capital, they expanded their cattle herd to about 2,000 head. However, the country was rapidly being settled and the range on the Tongue River was becoming constricted. In 1884 they moved the ranch to Otter Creek, which was practically uninhabited, and established the present-day Circle Bar Ranch. All the partners applied for Desert Land entry claims, as did the sons when they came of age, thereby accumulating several miles of Otter Creek bottom land. From this base and thousands of acres of public grassland, the ranch rapidly grew into a cattle herd of about 8,000 head and a considerable horse herd.[6] Of the three boys, Gus, Levi, and Robert, Levi most embraced the livestock business. All the boys worked actively on the ranch and were educated by their mother before being sent East for additional education in their late teens. However, Robert elected not to return to Montana upon completion of his formal education in the East. Gus started his own ranch but later sold out to Captain Joe T. Brown of the Three Circle Ranch and left the area. When Captain Howes retired and moved back to Dennis, Massachusetts, Levi Howes was given his father's homestead and became the driving force of the Circle Bar. Eventually he bought Gus Howes' old holdings from Captain Brown and put all the Circle Bar back together.

By 1900 Levi Howes was clearly in complete charge of the Circle Bar. He had fully consolidated the family holdings and purchased several additional homesteads from failing families. More importantly, he had grown into the active leadership role necessary to become the most influential voice in the Otter community. As a result of his ability to handle stock and men, he had the complete respect of the tough cowboys-turned-ranchers who were his neighbors. With the capital, education, political contacts, and personality, Levi Howes was clearly a force to be reckoned with when Selway tried to enter the Otter Creek drainage.

---

[6] Howes, *Montana Territory.*

Figure 25: Levi Howes' Circle Bar Ranch (L.A. Huffman), courtesy of the Montana Historical Society.

It was Levi Howes who first warned John Daut not to bring Selway sheep onto the Otter Creek range. Daut reported he was met by Levi Howes and three other cattlemen with the warning. According to Daut, Levi stated that he represented a "settler's committee" of seventeen landowners who opposed the Selway sheep.[7] When this warning was followed by the stampeding of 300 Circle Bar horses through Daut's herd twice in November 1900, it was clear that Levi Howes was taking action. While not an active participant in the actual raid, to assume that Levi Howes was not involved strains all credibility.

In his memoirs *Montana Territory*, Howes revealed that the settlement with Daut amounted to $4,000, which was raised by subscription. Although it was John B. Kendrick who made Daut the initial offer of a settlement, there had to be a significant amount of

---

[7] Beach, *Faded Hoof Prints—Bygone Dreams*, John Daut's Story.

coordination to determine the amount and allocation of the sub-scription. Kendrick had volunteered that he might contribute up to $1,000 only if other cattlemen would agree to the terms. Since Levi Howes was the head of the Committee, he had to be inti-mately involved in planning the raid, the terms of the settlement, and the collection of the subscription money.

CHAPTER TEN

THE QUIET HELPERS

Three and possibly four cattlemen other than Kendrick and Brewster were important active participants in the raid.

CHARLES THEX

Figure 26: Charlie Thex and his wife Bertha on their wedding in 1897.

First and probably most important of these accomplices was the old-time Texas gunman Charles Thex. A fascinating figure, Charlie Thex was the consummate intimidating presence necessary to convince the sheep men that the cattlemen were deadly serious. In 1877 Thex was a mere lad of sixteen named Sheely Scott, who joined a trail herd in Texas bound for Montana.[1] He completed the drive and turned the cattle loose at Telegraph Point in Montana. Telegraph Point was a telegraph station between Fort Mead at Sturgis in South Dakota and Fort Keogh in Miles City, Montana, that grew into a small town named Stoneville, later named Alzada.

Sheely Scott and an older member of the trail crew decided they would hunt buffalo, which were numerous between Telegraph Point and Miles City. The following winter they hunted up and down the Powder River, Otter Creek, and the Tongue River, collecting hides that they sold in Miles City at a good price in the spring.

They decided to return to Texas by way of Deadwood, South Dakota, but stopped at Telegraph Point, which was now called Stoneville. His partner joined a poker game and was losing heavily when he caught a professional gambler cheating. The gambler shot and killed his partner, whereupon Sheely Scott shot and killed the gambler.[2] Leaving Stoneville quickly with his and his partner's horses, Sheely started back to Texas.

Arriving in northern Texas, he met and joined a group of men that included some Texas Rangers. They were pursuing a group of Comanche Indians who had been raiding in the area. They overtook the Indians and engaged them, with Sheely credited with three kills. He stayed with the Texas Rangers for about six months before returning to his home in central Texas.

Home in Texas, the area was still controlled by the U.S. Army under the Reconstruction Act. Sheely and a friend got into a fight at a "darky" drinking establishment that resulted in the death of

---

[1] Interview and correspondence with Neil Thex, 2016–2018.
[2] Interview and correspondence with Neil Thex, 2016–2018.

several black patrons.[3] Fearing the U.S. Army, Sheely and his friend fled north and west, and Sheely Scott changed his name to Charles the X, which became Charles Thex. They joined a trail herd going to Arizona. Upon completion of the job, the pair separated, and Charlie traveled by night and hid out during the day to avoid Apaches. Joining another trail herd in Indian Territory (Oklahoma), Charlie found himself paid off in Ogallala, Nebraska, a couple of months later.

Remembering the beautiful Otter Creek country, Charlie decided to head that direction and arrived back in Miles City, Montana, looking for work. He found work with the N Bar and then with Lord "Noll" Wallop on his horse ranch on Otter Creek. Thereafter he worked for about seven years with the Circle Bar before he bought the John Edwards place on Otter Creek and started his own ranch. (John Edwards was reportedly a member of Stuart's Stranglers, the vigilante group that killed sixty-three outlaws throughout eastern Montana in the summer of 1884.)

One incident on Otter Creek before the sheep killing involved the theft of about 200 head of cattle from Charlie and his neighbors by a man named Archie Carnes. Charlie and his neighbors caught the cow thief on the Powder River.[4] Charlie held the thief at gunpoint while the group decided his fate. Charlie's vote was to tie a hangman's noose in his saddle rope and throw it over a cottonwood limb. The rest of the group, however, "chickened out" on the hanging. Much to Charlie Thex's disgust, the group voted to give the man a rope beating and set him afoot.[5]

On another occasion, some horses were stolen from his corral. He trailed the two horse thieves, killed one, and sent the other, a teenager, on his way with the advice that if he saw him again he would kill him on sight.

It is no wonder that when guns were drawn at the beginning of the Bear Creek Raid, Charlie Thex was the man holding the

---

[3] Interview and correspondence with Neil Thex, 2016–2018.
[4] Interview and correspondence with Neil Thex, 2016–2018.
[5] Ibid.

gun on the herder, Dan Squires. Total intimidation was essential to the success of the operation, and Charlie Thex was the picture of intimidation. It is entirely possible that Dan Squires recognized Charlie Thex despite his gunnysack mask and knew better than to offer resistance. When Charlie told him to leave the country and not come back, he did exactly as he was told.

Charlie Thex became a very successful cattleman on Otter Creek. He bought land when it was cheap and at one point had nearly 2,000 head of cattle, which he later sold to Captain Brown of the Three Circle. He was one of the raid's last survivors and died in 1954 at the age of ninety-three.[6]

HORTON SINCLAIR BOAL

Figure 27: Horton Boal, courtesy of the American Heritage Center.

Horton Boal was the son-in-law of W. F. "Buffalo Bill" Cody. He married Arta Cody, first child of W. F. Cody and briefly served as the manager of the "Scout's Rest" ranch in North Platte, Nebraska.

---

[6] Beach, *Faded Hoof Prints—Bygone Dreams*; Charles Thex Family and Maude Beach interviews; grandson Neil Thex interviews.

He had a disagreement with his father-in-law about ranch management and moved to Sheridan, Wyoming, in 1893 when Cody built the Sheridan Inn.[7] Boal established a ranch near Sheridan, and Arta looked after her father's interests and assisted in the establishment of the inn. In 1900 they sold the Sheridan ranch and reestablished his Three X Bar Ranch on the East Fork of Hanging Woman Creek in Montana. He built a comfortable house, bunkhouse, barns, and corrals. Over the next two years Boal went deeply into debt buying cattle at the top of the market.[8]

The availability of abundant public grazing land was critical to the success of his business. As a late member of the Committee, he saw the Daut and Selway invasion as a clear and present danger to his ranching enterprise. He was probably approached by Kendrick and Brewster to provide his ranch as a staging point for the raid. It was strategically located on the East Fork of Hanging Woman Creek only a few miles from the Daut and Selway flocks and off any highly traveled roads. It also had a bunkhouse and barns large enough to support a force of eleven men and their horses, where they could gather the group, make final plans, and be at the raid site early on the morning of December 28, 1900.

Following the raid, Horton Boal's cattle operation was decimated by low cattle prices.[9] Faced with mounting financial problems, he was forced to liquidate his herd at an inopportune time and suffered heavy losses. Also, in 1902 he encountered marital problems, and his wife and two children left the Three X Bar and moved to Kansas City. In a final blow, his mother died a few days later. He was overtaken by depression[10] and committed suicide by inhaling chloroform from his shoe at the (Historic) Sheridan Inn on October 27, 1902. He was only forty years old.

Interestingly, Kendrick's attorney W. S. Metz handled the estate, and John B. Kendrick, George Brewster, and J. H. "Shorty"

---

[7]   Atkins, *Reflections of the Inn.*
[8]   Probate documents of Horton Sinclair Boal, Rosebud County, Montana.
[9]   "Gone on His Last Roundup," *Billings Gazette*, October 31, 1902.
[10] Atkins, *Reflections of the Inn.*

Cadell were appointed as appraisers for the estate. They arranged for the sale of the remaining livestock, ranch equipment, and sale of the ranch.[11]

FRANK "BOOKER" LACY

Frank "Booker" Lacy was born in Zamhill, Oregon, on June 12, 1867, as one of twelve children. His family left Oregon and moved first to Texas and then to Nebraska where his father homesteaded near Scottsbluff. At the age of seventeen he went to work for several large cattle companies in western Nebraska and eastern Wyoming.[12] He joined the Converse Cattle Company at Lance Creek while John B. Kendrick was superintendent and came to Montana when Kendrick moved from Lance Creek near Lusk, Wyoming, to the OW on Hanging Woman Creek. Lacy worked sixteen years for Kendrick, who had a high level of respect for Lacy's management acumen and loyalty.[13]

While Booker was a legendary scrooge, he was also a very perceptive businessman. He carefully saved every cent he earned and invested in land and cattle on Lower Hanging Woman Creek. While continuing to work for Kendrick, Lacy started with a homestead on "Lacy Gulch" and steadily built his cow herd. When his operation grew to a sufficient size, he left Kendrick's employ to concentrate on his own business. However, he and Kendrick remained close friends and often shared work on roundups, brandings, and social gatherings. Directly threatened by Selway's entry on the Otter Creek range and Daut's homestead at the head of Tooley Creek, Booker Lacy was an easy recruit for John B. Kendrick's Bear Creek Raid.

Booker Lacy eventually built a ranch of almost a township in size. In 1919 he sold his cattle, totaling about 1,500 head, to "Doc" Spear for the grand sum of $100,000. Thereafter he became the "banker of Birney," lending money to a number of local residents. He funded

11 Probate documents of Horton Sinclair Boal, Rosebud County, Montana.
12 Frank Lacy interview with Bob Helvey.
13 King, *The Empire Builders*.

the founding of "Bones Brother's" Dude Ranch and partnered with Mamie Nance in starting the Birney Ranch Store. In 1940 he sold his land holdings to Ned and Libby Cox and retired to Sheridan, Wyoming. He lived well into his nineties and died July 27, 1964.[14]

While never admitting that he participated in the Bear Creek Raid, Lacy did provide a few fascinating details about the raid to Bob Helvey in an interview in 1960. In that interview, he revealed that the reason the herd of ewe lambs was selected for slaughter was because their skulls were not fully formed and therefore more easily killed by clubbing. Also, the death of elite replacement ewes would slow Daut's expansion in the area.

A humorous story about Booker Lacy's famous skinflint ways has come down through oral history.[15] One evening a cowboy came to his house to visit him about some business, and they were conversing by candlelight. Booker said to the cowboy, "I guess we don't need light to talk about this," and extinguished the candle to save money. The cowboy promptly removed his pants and they continued talking. When Booker relit the candle, the cowboy put his pants back on. An astonished Booker said, "Why in hell did you take your pants off?" The cowboy replied, "Well, I didn't want to wear out the bottom of my Levis and it didn't matter since we were sitting in the dark."

Another story involved Booker Lacy and "Bill" Munson's wife at a Birney dance. Mrs. Munson teasingly asked Booker, "How did such a small man like you swing such a big club on that sheep raid?" It is reported that Lacy replied, "Why Mrs. Munson, I didn't swing any clubs, I was too busy carrying water to your husband." Such are the stories that have come down as oral history.[16]

---

14 Helvey/Lacy interview, July 23, 1957.

15 Interview with Arthur Hays Jr., great-grandson of Captain Joe T. Brown, March 2018.

16 Note: This story was first reported in chapter 3 of *Before Barbed Wire*, in which the informant asked author Brown not to reveal her name. In a Floyd Alderson transcript of an interview with Maime "Peachy" Cox, she tells the same story but with her informant being her cousin Fay Humphries. In the first story the husband's name was "William" and in the second the husband's name was "Nat." It is this author's belief that the husband was "Bill" Munson, but Maime Cox heard the story from Fay Humphries.

BARNA HALL

Figure 28: Barnabas C. Hall.

The 1900 census lists Barnabas Hall as a resident of the Otter Creek area.[17] He homesteaded at the junction of Bear and Otter Creeks, making him the most impacted of the landowning participants of the Bear Creek Raid. He was a cousin of Levi Howes, the nephew of Levi's mother, Sarah Freeman (Hall) Howes. Barna left the area in 1913 to return to Massachusetts.

THE COWBOYS

John B. Kendrick brought four of his most trusted "hands" to provide manpower for the Bear Creek Raid. All four had come with Kendrick and Lacy from the Converse Cattle Company at Lusk, Wyoming. It should be noted that Lusk was near several of the large cattle outfits that had been involved in the Johnson County War. These were men who had represented, or "repped," for Converse Cattle Company with the neighboring ranches. Some of the men they would have known were George (Kid) Curry and

---

[17] 1900 Federal Census Records of School District 01, Custer County, Montana.

Mike Shonsey, both straw bosses of the nearby Fiddleback Ranch. Curry became the most vicious killer in the famous Wild Bunch, and Mike Shonsey was a "stock detective" with the Wyoming Stock Growers who was implicated in the murders of Nate and Dud Champion during the Johnson County War. While Kendrick left Lusk two years before the "War," he brought with him men familiar with frontier violence.

WILLIAM "BILL" MUNSON

Bill Munson was born in Georgetown, Texas, on March 25, 1865, and came with the Wulfjen Cattle Co. to Wyoming on a trail herd in 1886. He began his association with John B. Kendrick when he was working at the original Converse Cattle Company and Kendrick was the managing superintendent. When Kendrick moved the company to Hanging Woman Creek, Munson came with the herd. He rose to become the wagon boss of the OW Ranch and had a homestead on Lee Creek. At the time of the Bear Creek Raid, Munson was one of Kendrick's most loyal employees. His homestead was also in close proximity to the land that Daut had chosen as his homestead. Shortly after the raid, Munson left the OW employ, sold his homestead on Lee Creek, and moved to an irrigated farm at Decker, Montana, passing away in 1951.[18]

FRANK MCKINNEY

Frank McKinney also came to the OW with the original Kendrick herd from Lusk. He became foreman of the OW and at the time of the raid was considered a loyal employee. However, the year following the raid, he was somehow involved in the death of another employee in a horse accident and left the OW. He is strangely missing from recorded OW history. He later homesteaded on the Tongue River and had ranches at Kirby and Squirrel Creek

---

[18] Obituary, *The Sheridan Press*, January 8, 1951.

Figure 29: Frank McKinney with Nannie Alderson.

in Montana. He then moved to LaGrande, Oregon, where he retired. He died in Pendleton, Oregon, at the age of eighty-nine.[19]

WALT SNIDER

Walt Snider was still another OW cowboy who came with the original cow herd from Lusk. He had a homestead about halfway between the OW and Daut's homestead. In addition to working for the OW he also ran a few cows. For a while he served as the postmaster of the short-lived community of Gofer.[20] In later years he was awarded a lucrative lease on the "Ceded Strip" that Kendrick had purchased on the Crow Reservation.[21]

MAHLON "TUG" WILSON

Mahlon C. "Tug" Wilson was born on May 16, 1855, in Hamilton County, Indiana, but soon moved to Texas. He came up the trail with a herd of cattle to Lusk, Wyoming, for the Converse Cattle Company, where he met John B. Kendrick. Wilson came to the OW

---

[19] Interview with William "Bill" McKinney, grandson of Frank McKinney.
[20] *They Came and They Stayed*, Rosebud County History.
[21] King, *The Empire Builders.*

Figure 30: Mahlon "Tug" Wilson, courtesy of the Trail End State Historic Site (Harmon Collection).

Ranch in Montana with Kendrick and the original Kendrick herd. Perhaps the most loyal of the Kendrick employees, he worked for John B. Kendrick his entire working life. He served as the wagon boss of the OW and only left the ranch when he became too frail to live there. He died in Sheridan, Wyoming, at the age of eighty-six. He never married.[22]

J. H. "SHORTY" CADDEL

Figure 31: Shorty Caddel.

Shorty Caddel was the youngest participant (age twenty-six) in the raid and the only one who was not a hard-bitten veteran.

Although employed during the raid by Horton Boal, Caddel was later a loyal employee of George Brewster and worked for him on and off for several years. He was the last surviving participant of the raid and the only one who gave an eyewitness account of the historic event. Just before everyone else had died, he told the story

---

22 King, *The Empire Builders.*

to Lyman Brewster, son of George Brewster, one of the leaders of the raid. Brewster waited until Shorty Caddel had passed and then preserved the event with a short account in the fall 1974 issue of *Montana: The Magazine of Western History.*

Shorty worked for several ranches in the raid area including the Three X Bar, Quarter Circle U, and the Spear outfit. He homesteaded on the South Fork of Canyon Creek in Rosebud County, Montana, and spent his later years in Wyola, Montana. He passed away on May 21, 1966.[23]

---

[23] Helvey/Caddel interview; also Caddel's obituary in *The Sheridan Press.*

SO WHAT REALLY HAPPENED
A Scenario

So what really happened at the Bear Creek Raid? One can shrug his shoulders and say, "I don't know," or examine the evidence and provide a probable scenario. Building a scenario necessarily involves a degree of speculation but is largely informed by facts. The following is this author's scenario:

In October 1900 Levi Howes noted the arrival of sheep man John Daut in the Otter Creek area. Daut announced that he was looking to exercise his homestead rights in the vicinity. Homesteaders had been moving in and out of the area for years and no one thought much about it. Daut filed on a good spring on Tooley Creek and began building a small house, a set of corrals, and other improvements.

All of this was normal activity until the arrival of a surveyor and his assistant from Miles City. When the surveyors were observed staying at Daut's house but surveying another spring far beyond his homestead boundary, Levi demanded the men tell him for whom they were working. The head surveyor replied that he was surveying seventy-two forty-acre parcels for R. R. "Bob" Selway, which were to be purchased with script in addition to two desert claims for Daut and his wife.

When Levi Howes heard the name Selway, he immediately knew that his range was under attack. Selway was one of the largest sheep owners in the state of Montana and controlled the Pumpkin Creek drainage, which was the next major drainage north of Otter Creek. Ownership of seventy-two forty-acre parcels on water meant control over 50,000 acres of adjacent public land in the heart of his range. This was an existential threat to his ranch and that of his neighbors John B. Kendrick, Horton Boal, Frank Lacy, and his cousin, Barna Hall. He knew Selway would probably not stop with this incursion, but if allowed to stay would endanger the whole cattle industry in the area.

He immediately notified his neighbors of the threat and organized for action. Around November 1, 1900, he confronted John Daut and asked him directly if he intended to bring in sheep. When Daut replied that he thought he could put any livestock he wanted on his own land, Levi told him he could put whatever he wanted on his homestead, but that the public range was closed to sheep.

Levi pointed out that range customs had already determined that Otter Creek was cattle country by first use and Selway was violating "range orders" if Daut and Selway tried to bring in sheep. When Daut replied that "range orders" had no legal validity, Levi Howes warned him that he and his neighbors would defend their range at all costs.

Levi Howes then reactivated the Otter Creek Defenders to oppose the potential Selway invasion and reached out to Kendrick, Lacy, Boal, Brewster, and Brown in the Hanging Woman and Tongue River area. Captain Joe T. Brown, as the commander of Company C of the Montana State Militia, declined to participate because he felt he couldn't be involved in what might evolve into extralegal activity.[1] Captain Brown was dropped from further planning and was not apprised of any pending actions. George Brewster felt no such restriction due to his close relation to John B. Kendrick.

Early in the month of November, Daut began moving 8,500 head of sheep in two bands from Pumpkin Creek. The sheep were trailed slowly but inexorably toward Otter Creek. Levi Howes had

---

[1] Interview with Arthur Hayes, Jr.

scouts watching the progress, and when the sheep crossed west of the "deadline" on Bradshaw Creek, word went out to the cattlemen that sheep had crossed the line. They prepared for action.

A meeting was held between Howes, Kendrick, and Brewster to plan what needed to occur to try and discourage the incursion. Kendrick wanted to make sure Howes was fully committed to action due to his previous experience with Howes in the Johnson County War. At the same time, he did not want any human deaths or injuries that would result in legal action.

When the sheep bands camped just above the Circle Bar Ranch and then passed the next day in full view of his house, Levi Howes determined to act. He directed his hands to gather 300 head of horses and keep them off water for two days. By the end of that time, two bands of sheep were on Tooley Creek: The larger band was at Daut's homestead and the smaller on a spring near the mouth of Tooley Creek. When the sheep were brought back to the waterhole that evening, the 300 head of thirsty horses were stampeded through the smaller herd.[2] About thirty sheep were killed and many more injured. It took a couple of days for Daut to gather the scattered band and reorganize the flock. The cattlemen had demonstrated that they were deadly serious.

Daut's wife was frantic at the news of the attack and begged her husband to go back to Pumpkin Creek where it was safe and they had a nice house. Despite his wife's concerns, Daut felt that he was legally in the right and remained committed to the venture. He took the precaution of arming the two herders and the camp tender and moved the larger herd from his house to Bear Creek. He instructed his herders not to shoot at any cowboys except in self-defense. A week later the larger herd was attacked in the same manner, with stampeding horses and yelling cowboys. There was no shooting, but again several sheep were injured or killed. Daut's wife again implored him to leave, but Daut was no coward.

By this time it was the first day of December and Daut showed

---

2 Leota Kimes Dunning interview with Bob Helvey.

Figure 32: Horton Boal's Three X Bar Ranch (L. A. Huffman), courtesy of the Montana Historical Society (this picture was labeled simply "Bowles Ranch" with no further identifiers).

no signs of leaving. Levi met with the Committee and decided to post a final warning. A note in big block letters from the Committee telling Daut to move his sheep east of Bradshaw Creek or they would all be killed was nailed to Dan Squires' sheep wagon.

The next four weeks were a period of calm for the sheep men and heavy planning for the cattlemen. The leaders met again and decided they would have to destroy the sheep. Howes did not want to expose his men to any more overt action, fearing that many of them could be identified already. Kendrick agreed and suggested that most of the men could come from Hanging Woman, but he wanted some representation from Otter Creek, and he wanted Charlie Thex in case they faced serious gunplay. Since they needed a place to meet that was off the beaten path, they asked Horton Boal if they could use the Three X Bar and he assented. It was far off any highly traveled roads, centrally located, and had the facilities for a dozen or so men. Since Kendrick wanted to tightly control the operation, he chose most of the raiding crew from his veteran cowboys, plus George Brewster. Horton Boal and Shorty Caddel were selected because they would be leaving from the Three X Bar and would know about the operation already. That left just Charlie Thex and Barna Hall to represent Otter Creek.

The raid was originally scheduled for December 27 but had to be postponed until December 28 to accommodate George Brewster. Levi Howes had members of the Committee posted on upper and lower Otter Creek, upper Bear Creek, and the roads between Tooley Creek and the OW Ranch to prevent unwanted travelers from blundering into the raid.

Before daylight the raiders left the Three X Bar and rode the eight miles to the mouth of Tooley Creek. As described by Shorty Caddel, Charlie Thex drew his gun on the herder, made him serve the group coffee, and then tied him to the wagon wheel. They then went after the sheep.

It would take at least two riders and probably three to hold the herd under the cut bank. Two teams of three men each, one roper on horseback and two ground men with clubs, likely did the killing. The ropers would catch a sheep around the head and drag it between the two club men like a calf to the branding fire. During the "drag" the sheep would be "choked down," resulting in less struggling by the time it reached the ground men, thus presenting a much easier target. Two bats to the head would usually be enough to dispatch the animal. The ropers would then drag the dispatched sheep to the dead pile, where the remaining two men would take off the ropes. The ropers would return to the live herd for another trip. This procedure avoided the problems of crippled sheep and panicked horses trying to avoid stampeding sheep.

Since they left the sheep camp before dark, given the short winter days the killers would have had to average two head per minute for ten hours. This would have been extremely hard work. Furthermore, there must have been an occasional break for water or coffee and to let the herder loose to walk around a little so he didn't freeze to death. These men were very careful not to kill or injure the herder so there would only be a damage claim for lost sheep and not a capital criminal case. Kendrick felt this was important for public relations; he wanted most people in the area to view

Figure 33: Charlie Thex's Colt pistol, courtesy of the Bull Family.

the result positively or at least with neutrality. Even if they didn't approve of the tactics used, they could applaud Selway's departure from the area. (However, after the event Captain Brown voiced his disapproval of the raid in no uncertain terms.)

Afterward, the raiders attended the "alibi" dances held over the New Year's holiday at the 4D Ranch owned by Nat Humphries[3] and at Kendrick's OW. George Brewster probably set up the 4D Ranch dance with Nat Humphries even though he was Captain Brown's brother-in-law. It was not unusual for such an event to take place at the 4D because it was set up for entertaining, and the Birney community was always up for a party.[4] It was reported that Charlie Thex played the fiddle at the OW, and George Brewster and Shorty Caddel were both seen at the 4D.

Although the sheepherder, Dan Squires, left the area immediately after the raid, in later years he returned to the Powderville

---

[3] Irving Alderson, Jr., interviews with Forest Dunning, 2018.
[4] Maime "Peachy" Cox interview with Floyd Alderson.

area and worked for the LO Ranch.[5] He consistently refused to talk about the incident (possibly due to fear of Charlie Thex). He died in Miles City in 1911.

One of the characteristics of the raid that met with great approval was the fact that there were no injuries to any humans in the incident. Because the losses were damages that could be mitigated by money, the offer by cattlemen to raise a damage settlement by subscription offset most of the criticism. It also went a long way toward preserving the "conspiracy of silence." Silence did not necessarily apply to conversations between the participants and their wives, so the wives knew what had happened but were not going to say anything that would implicate their husbands. However, that didn't prevent them from talking among themselves or with participants other than their husbands. Through that channel much of the general outline of what happened became generally known throughout the communities, though the details were closely held. Nonetheless, in the eyes of the local and larger community, the Bear Creek Raid was generally viewed positively.

---

[5] Brown and Felton, *Before Barbed Wire*.

CHAPTER TWELVE

SHEEP RAIDS DONE RIGHT
AND WRONG

W hy did the Montana Vigilantes escape history with a generally favorable rating, while Wyoming seemed to get it wrong
time after time? Montana had a relatively positive experience with
the practice, while in Wyoming the practice led to the disasters of
the Johnson County War and the Spring Creek Sheep Raid.

The answer to that question lies in two factors—timing and
leadership. In the early years of the frontier when there was no effective law enforcement in either of the two states, vigilante justice
was nearly the only defense against lawlessness. In the Montana
goldfields, the rise of the Plummer Gang in 1865–66 proved that
the territorial and local authorities were ineffective in protecting
the public. The distances involved, the paucity of federal marshals,
and the local intimidation of voters by Sheriff Plummer combined
to produce a public outrage. Under the excellent leadership of
good men like Granville Stuart, vigilance committees were formed
and dealt with the worst offenders. About sixty-five of the most
vicious criminals were shot or hanged, including Sheriff Plummer,
and many others banished from the camps. Relative peace and
tranquility were restored, and honest local authorities elected.
Similar experiences also occurred in Cheyenne, Laramie, and other
newly formed Wyoming communities in the 1870s.

Unfortunately, the positive experiences of the early vigilante days created a mindset that vigilantism was a panacea to be used whenever someone felt wronged. This attitude persisted long after a reasonably good legal system was in place throughout both states.

In Montana the public order again came under attack with the rise of outlaw gangs in the early 1880s, which involved mostly horse theft. This led to the establishment of the Montana Stock Growers Association, which included both sheep and cattle operators. Horse thieves were a universal problem. The Montana association was open to all stock growers, both large and small, and thereby avoided most of the "big versus little" conflicts prevalent in Wyoming. When the association's executive committee decided to form a "direct action" team in the spring of 1884, they turned to the old goldfield veteran, Granville Stuart, to command the team. With a small, highly organized group of fifteen vigilantes, Stuart's Stranglers swept through eastern Montana in the summer of 1884 and shot or hanged sixty-three outlaws along the Missouri and Yellowstone Rivers. While the action was met with some criticism at the time, the salutatory effect of a major drop in crime soon quieted the critics. The Stranglers' success served as a template for the Wyoming Stock Growers Association's ill-fated "invasion" of Johnson County in Wyoming eight years later in 1892.

When John B. Kendrick led the successful 1900 Bear Creek Raid that stopped sheep men from entering the Otter Creek country in southeast Montana, he may have inadvertently reinforced the mindset that the old vigilante model could be used in Wyoming. A series of sheep raids between 1905 and 1909 in Wyoming's Big Horn Basin resulted in at least two murders prior to the historic Spring Creek Raid, which killed three sheep men and set the stage for a trial that finally broke the back of vigilantism in Wyoming.

If we contrast the vigilante actions in the two states, it's important to note that the timing of the Montana activities preceded the Wyoming incidents by five to eight years. Except for the Kendrick Raid, most of the Montana vigilante incidents took place prior to statehood. In addition, the general public in Montana felt threatened by crime, as opposed to one faction or the other appearing to use violence to advance its economic interests. Both Wyoming incidents occurred after the state had been organized and there were fights over control of the public range.

In addition, the passage of time meant that the rule of law was more established when the influx of homesteaders diluted the potential jury pools, which heretofore had been likely to contain partisans from one side or the other. "Hung" juries in range fights were common before the arrival of homesteaders because, given the limited population for jury pools, a random jury selection was likely to include partisans from both sides, resulting in jury indecision.

Perhaps even more important than the passage of time was the quality of vigilante leadership between the two states. In Montana both major vigilante actions before statehood were heavily influenced by Granville Stuart, an early Montana pioneer who helped organize the first Montana Vigilantes. Stuart was a unique individual who had a strong sense of right and wrong. He was active in the early formation of the state's mining and ranching industries and had a statewide reputation for fair play. He learned early in the 1865–66 cleanup that tight control of the target selection process and the recruitment of vigilante fighters were keys to a successful operation. He later admitted that in the 1865–66 operations, there were a few men killed who were not "worst of the worst" but only loosely connected to the outlaws. Therefore, during the 1884 operation, he publicly opposed the "direct action" proposed by Teddy Roosevelt and the Marquis de Mores at the 1884 Montana Stock Growers convention. However, as part of the executive committee he personally led a group of fifteen hand-picked men in the execution of sixty-three horse thieves and ruffians, including some related to prominent families. Because the selection process was so accurate, and the executions so tightly controlled, the action received the support of the public.

Likewise, when John B. Kendrick led the Bear Creek Raid, he assembled a group that was under his iron-fisted control. They were mostly fellow stock owners and veteran cowboys who had been with him for years. Careful not to injure the sheepherder or burn his wagon, the raiders only killed the sheep. After the raid he, Levi Howes, and the other planners made sure that cattlemen offered compensation to Daut and Selway and gave them time to move the remainder of their sheep to unoccupied range. There were no "loose cannons" rolling around the decks of this Montana vigilante operation.

In the short term, Kendrick's raid probably proved to be even more widely successful in Montana than the raiders intended. Within the next three months there were successful threats communicated to sheep men on the Powder River and in Deer Lodge County.

On the Powder River, a note was stapled to a sheep wagon at a Hank Greenway camp that said:

DON'T BRING YOUR SHEEP TO POWDER RIVER,

IF YOU DO, BRING YOUR COFFIN.

YOU WILL NEED IT.

While Greenway was not discouraged by the threat, he did meet with fellow cattlemen in the area and agreed to draw demarcation lines between himself and his cattle neighbors.

In Deer Lodge County, the following message was published:

> Custer county is not the only one in Montana which has troubles between some of the sheep men and some of the cattle men. In Deer Lodge county the cattle men own or lease nearly all the range and a number of sheep men having unloaded their stock on the cattle men's territory, the latter have informed them in an open letter published by Representative Geary that if they find a sheep or any number of sheep anywhere between the Big Blackfoot and the north fork of that stream any time after the 15th day of April, Anno Domini 1901, they will make the brand very scarce. The letter concludes: "We are not desperate until we try ·until we are driven to it. We may as well die as be starved out. Don't be in doubt as to who the author is. I'll be captain.
> "MIKE GEARY."

Figure 34: Yellowstone Journal, *April 11, 1901.*

Sheep men refrained from moving into the Deer Lodge range.

In Wyoming the actors could not have been more different. There the Wyoming Stock Growers Association (WYSGA) restricted the membership of their organization to large cattle operators, including John B. Kendrick. Using their financial and political power, "big ranchers" gained control of the state government and used that power for their own narrow interests. When the ownership question of "mavericks" arose, the WYSGA defined the law to bar nonmembers from ownership of unbranded cattle. This effectively made outlaws of hundreds of honest small cattlemen when they branded a maverick. In the meantime, WYSGA members were paying their cowboys two to five dollars a head to put their own brand on similar livestock. This was unacceptable in Johnson County, which by 1892 had been largely settled by small cattle and sheep men. When the WYSGA tried to enforce the state law in Johnson County, they failed to garner convictions because jury pools were filled with small operators who "hung" the juries. Local Johnson County political figures, including the sheriff, reflected the views of their voters.

In April 1892 the WYSGA decided to "clean up" Johnson County by extralegal means. Using the model pioneered by Granville Stuart, they outfitted a vigilante force of fifty men and "invaded" Johnson County with the express intent to kill a list of small cattlemen they deemed rustlers and the local politicians that supported them.

However, unlike Stuart's fifteen hand-picked men, half of the "vigilantes" were gunmen imported from Texas who had little in common with Wyoming citizens. The other half were highly partisan large cattlemen and their managers. Selected for leadership were two firebrands, Major Frank Walcott and Billy Irwin, neither of whom intimately knew the men they were supposed to control. The operation fell apart due to weather, dissention between the Texans and the Wyoming ranchers, and an aroused public. After killing Nate Champion and Nick Ray at the KC Ranch, the Johnson County "Invaders" were surrounded at the TA Ranch by

300 to 400 small cattlemen and townspeople and had to be rescued by the U.S. Army from Fort McKinney. Unfortunately, the "Invaders" escaped justice due to WYSGA political influence, but in the following election cycle the people of Wyoming spoke and the WYSGA's power in state government was sharply reduced.

Following the disaster of the Johnson County War, the state of Wyoming was relatively quiet and good progress was made toward the rule of law, but there continued to be fights over the "range rights" to federal grazing. Most of the conflict came from a changing demographic as more and more homesteaders (small farmers) moved onto farmable land and gained legal title. This displaced cattle and sheep interests grazing the public land. As the available public land decreased, competition for the remaining land increased. Cattlemen and sheep men began to push each other's traditional "deadlines" between livestock holders, which had been the range custom.

Nowhere in Wyoming was this conflict starker than the Big Horn Basin. As major irrigation projects converted grazing land to farms, the remaining productive public grazing land decreased rapidly. With the increase in small farmers with private holdings, the political power of both sheep men and cattlemen depending on public grazing was reduced. Sheep men, especially, began to be squeezed between the advancing farmers and the "lines of demarcation" that separated traditional cattle and sheep ranges. They responded by violating these customary "lines of demarcation," which had no basis in law. Cattlemen, with their livelihoods under attack, responded violently to protect their interests. A series of violent incidents beginning in 1903 between cattlemen and sheep men resulted in the deaths of Ben Minnick and Louis Gantz, and the severe wounding of Lincoln Morrison, all sheep men. Thousands of sheep were killed, and the perpetrators were never prosecuted.

In 1909 the issue again came to a boil with the infamous Spring Creek Raid, which resulted in the brutal deaths of sheep men Joe Allemand, Jules Lazier, and Joe Emge. With three men killed, their bodies burned, and hundreds of sheep killed, the ire of the community was raised to a fever pitch. This time the governor of Wyoming responded with total support for the local prosecutor; the sheriff conducted a thorough investigation; and five of the seven raiders were convicted of crimes ranging from arson to first degree murder. Two other participants who did not participate in the murders turned state's evidence because they had been promised by raid leaders that no humans would be killed. During the trial it was revealed that the raid was led by George Saban and Milton Alexander, who were both prominent ranchers. Saban was an experienced vigilante who was suspected of leading other sheep raids and a mob that lynched two murderers in the Basin, Wyoming, jail and killed a deputy county official.

Of the three remaining raiders, one was a hotheaded cowboy named Herbert Brink, who shot Joe Allemand when his hands were raised and said, "It's a hell of a time of night to come out with your hands up." Brink was sentenced to death and the other four were given prison sentences. However, within five years one had died of Rocky Mountain spotted fever, George Saban had escaped, and the other three, including Herbert Brink, were paroled. The paroles were issued by big cattleman governor Joseph Carey at the end of his term in December 1914. His replacement was another big cattleman, John B. Kendrick, who gave Milton Alexander a full pardon shortly before the end of his governorship. So ended the saga of the Spring Creek Sheep Raid.[1]

What are the similarities and differences between the Bear Creek and Spring Creek raids? Sheep raids tended to follow a specific pattern. They usually began with cattlemen laying claim to a tract of public land by "first use," sometimes years earlier than arrival by sheep men. To enforce their claim, cattlemen published a general description of the range they claimed to the general public, thereby establishing their "customary range." Later arrivals, whether cattlemen, sheep men, or homesteaders, met resistance upon

---

[1] The definitive work on the Spring Creek Raid is *A Vast Amount of Trouble* by John W. Davis. It was the author's primary source for information on the event.

initial entry. This typically began with a warning to the entering party. Since homesteaders clearly had a legally enforceable claim, they were usually allowed to enter. Cattlemen generally recognized each other's "range rights." Sheep men did not, and took the view that all parties were entitled to use of the public land.

Cattlemen then established a "deadline" beyond which sheep were not allowed to cross. Sheep men subsequently challenged the "deadline" by crossing it. Upon sheep crossing the line, the cattle-men issued a stern verbal warning, followed by a written warning to move back across the "deadline." If the warnings were ignored, harassment began in the form of fires, stampedes, sheep dog killing, etc. Lastly, there would be a full-blown raid in which substantial sheep and their herders were killed or injured.

First, the similarities between the raids. Both raids had their genesis in poor land management decisions by the U.S. government. If the government had organized a leasing system for its public lands, much of the conflict could have been avoided. It took until the 1934 Taylor Grazing Act for a rational system to be devised for ad-ministering federal land, today under control of the Bureau of Land Management. Leasing had been available for national forests and Indian reservations years before the Taylor Grazing Act. Without the assignment of specific public land to a specific lessee, there was bound to be conflict. Also, the patchwork of various homestead acts, script distributions, and designation of national parks, forests, monuments, and Indian lands all combined to cause federal land management confusion. The failure to properly survey public land prior to opening it for settlement was another contributing factor.

Both raids reflected the common biases of cattlemen toward the threat posed by sheep. This bias originated with transient, unscru-pulous sheep men in the Southwest who intensively overgrazed public lands as they slowly moved their huge flocks across wide areas, leaving damaged range in their wake. Therefore, while not fully based in fact, most cattlemen believed that sheep caused per-manent damage to the range, ruined waterholes, and by their mere presence disturbed cattle. It didn't help that many cowboys came up the trail from Texas and brought with them prejudices against anyone who wasn't white and a fluent English speaker. Many of the sheepherders were Mexican, Basque, Spanish, or French immigrants who were easy targets for harassment.

As a group, sheep men were more inclined to violate the customary "range rights" and demarcation lines than cattlemen because it was in their interest to do so. Most came later than cattlemen and had a transient history not tied to a specific tract of land. They liked to wander widely looking for the best feed for their flocks, which was not necessarily the same feed that cattle preferred. Most sheep men felt that cattle and sheep could coexist on the same range if it was not overstocked. They contended that "range rights" had no legal basis and they had as much right to the public range as cattlemen.

Though there was much in common between the two events, much was different. The first difference between the Bear Creek Raid and the Spring Creek Raid was the size and character of the opponents. In the Bear Creek incident, it was a clash of titans—Cattle King John B. Kendrick with thousands of cattle versus Sheep King Robert R. Selway with hundreds of thousands of sheep. In the Spring Creek Raid, it was relatively small cattlemen George Saban and Milton Alexander versus small sheep men Joe Allemand and Joe Emge. The presence of 8,500 sheep on Kendrick's and Howes' range was an irritant that had to be removed before it became serious because of Selway's size. The introduction of 5,000 sheep on Saban's and Alexander's range posed an imminent existential threat to their operations.

The timeline (1900) served Kendrick well in that the law in Custer County, Montana, was still mainly dominated by cattle interests, although that was changing rapidly. His raid was on the ragged edge of the "range rights"/strictly legal divide. Had his raid taken place one or two years later, the outcome might have been very different. In the Big Horn Basin, the nine years between 1900 and 1909 was a lifetime in terms of legal maturity. What was acceptable to the Wyoming public in 1905 was not by 1909.

Figure 35: Sheep Raid in Colorado, *drawn by Frenzesy* (Harpers Weekly).

Finally, there was the management of the actual raids. Kendrick planned and executed his raid with almost military precision. He briefed his raiders carefully. Charlie Thex was the only raider to draw a gun.[2] Under no circumstances except self-defense would the sheepherder be harmed. The sheep would be killed as a warning, but provisions would be made to pay for the sheep killed. The people invited on the raid were carefully chosen to avoid hotheads and extreme partisans. No burning of sheep wagons or other unnecessary violence would be tolerated. "Alibi" dances were planned so the raiders could be seen far from the scene. A "conspiracy of silence" was encouraged and supported by a committed community.

Contrast Kendrick's raid with that of George Saban and Milton Alexander. They picked a spot for the raid that was within eyesight of the Greet Ranch, where the raid was observed by witnesses.

---

2 Brewster, "December 1900: The Quiet Slaughter."

Discipline was broken when Herbert Brink opened fire and Joe Allemand was killed trying to surrender. Burning the sheep wagons, killing the dogs, and burning the bodies was all unnecessary violence, which inflamed public opinion against the raid. The raiders scattered back to their homes where some of them discussed the raid with family and friends. Lastly, the raiders were faced with a competent and willing prosecutor and sheriff encouraged by an irate public.[3]

Both raids slipped into history and legend. Bear Creek was dubbed "The Quiet Slaughter" and Spring Creek prompted the most famous criminal trial in the state of Wyoming. They could not have been more alike in genesis or more different in result.

---

[3] Davis, *A Vast Amount of Trouble.*

CHAPTER THIRTEEN

THE DAYS AFTER

In the early days after the Bear Creek Raid, Selway actively attempted to pursue the raiders through legal means. He offered big rewards for information in the local newspapers and pressured cattle-friendly Sheriff O. C. Cato to keep on the case. However, he found little success with Cato, who was not inclined to actively investigate the case since he had less than a month remaining on his term.[1] Also, the killing of a sheep in Custer County was only a misdemeanor punishable by sixty days in jail, so there was little political value in pursuing the matter.[2]

Selway then turned to the Montana Wool Growers Association and advocated larger rewards and harsher punishments for attacks on sheep wagons and flocks. When he lobbied his organization to post a $1,000 reward for information on the Bear Creek Raid participants, the county attorney volunteered to plead guilty and spend the sixty days in jail for the reward money since it was far in excess of his salary.[3] The idea was quickly withdrawn. However, Selway's more extreme actions were blocked by his fellow wool growers, who feared a generalized range war.

---

[1] Brown and Felton, *Before Barbed Wire*.
[2] *Yellowstone Journal*, April 17, 1901.
[3] "Wool Grower's Meeting," *Yellowstone Journal*, April 7, 1901, p. 8.

Selway believed that John B. Kendrick was the leader of the Committee, and he continued to try to use the law to bring him to justice. In 1906 the county attorney for Custer County used an affidavit of R. R. Selway and a statement from a supposed participant in the raid to charge John B. Kendrick with grand larceny for the events surrounding the raid. The case was dismissed on October 13, 1906. The probable cause for the dismissal was the disavowal of an affidavit by Jesse Bowe of South Dakota in which he stated that he was a participant in the Bear Creek Raid and named John B. Kendrick as the leader of the raid. In his disavowal, Mr. Bowe explained that "the Selway boys" had gotten him drunk in Belle Fourche and Spearfish, South Dakota, and while drunk he signed a paper in front of a notary. Given the length of time since the raid, lack of concrete evidence, and possible skullduggery by the Selway faction, the county attorney agreed to abandon the case.[4]

Interestingly, one of Kendrick's attorneys was W. S. Metz of Sheridan, Wyoming, the father of Percy Metz, the county attorney who successfully prosecuted the defendants in the Spring Creek Raid. W. S. Metz actually ran the Spring Creek prosecution team and assisted his son in achieving the most celebrated verdict in the history of Wyoming on November 11, 1909.[5] That verdict broke the back of vigilantism in Wyoming and the West. Yet it was W. S. Metz who defended John B. Kendrick against R. R. Selway's efforts to charge him criminally and civilly for the Bear Creek Raid beginning in 1901 and continuing until final dismissal in 1906. William Metz was also somewhat successful in the prosecution of another sheep raid case in Crook County, Wyoming, in April 1909.[6] Perhaps Metz the elder, although by all accounts an excellent attorney, developed his unique expertise in sheep cases while defending John B. Kendrick. If so, then ironically, Metz's defense of Montana vigilantism plowed the ground for its demise in Wyoming nine years later.

---

[4] State of Montana v. John B. Kendrick, Custer County court documents.
[5] Davis, *A Vast Amount of Trouble.*
[6] Davis, *Goodbye, Judge Lynch.*

Figure 36: William S. Metz, courtesy of the Sheridan County Courthouse.

Selway continued to pursue Kendrick and the other participants into later years. He offered numerous rewards that rose to as much as $19,000 for information that would lead to the arrest and conviction of the sheep killers. Unsubstantiated oral history claims that on one occasion he confronted John B. Kendrick in the First National Bank of Sheridan about his role in the raid. Kendrick grabbed him by the collar and threw him out into the street. Kendrick was never charged for his actions (it is good to be the king).

On another occasion Selway showed up drunk and waving a rifle on Charlie Thex's ranch. Dan Squires had named Thex to Daut as the man who probably held the pistol on him when the raid began. Nonetheless, Squires was not available to testify, and since the men all wore gunnysack masks, Thex could not be conclusively identified. Selway reportedly offered Thex $50,000 to turn state's evidence on John B. Kendrick. In an interview forty years later, Thex said the following conversation took place between Selway and himself: "Mr. Thex, I came here to have a confidential talk with you regarding those sheep. I believe there are those along this creek that could give information; and if you would turn state's evidence, I would make it worth your while up to $50,000."[7]

Neil Thex, Charlie's grandson, reported that Selway was drunk, talking wildly, and laid the rifle on the hood of his car while following Charlie around. Charlie got between Selway and the gun, grabbed it, and stuck the barrel in an old plow and bent it. He then handed the gun back to Selway. Forty years later Thex recalled this conversation in a Maude Beach interview: "Mr. Selway, I am in no need of any money at all, but if I were, I wouldn't take your proposition as I have never handled sheep, am not at all familiar with sheep and their diseases, and wouldn't know anything about the cause of their death, but if I did know anything about it, you nor your whole sheep association couldn't dig up enough money to hire me to tell it."[8]

After that exchange Selway left and Thex never heard from him again.

Selway's wife died during childbirth of his third child, and the other two children were given over to be raised by their grandparents.[9] Selway's behavior became more and more erratic with age, and he speculated wildly in all kinds of ventures. He suffered financial reversals and ultimately died a broken man.

John B. Kendrick continued to build his wealth and stature in the states of Montana and Wyoming. As previously noted, he became one of the wealthiest men in both states and got into politics. He served in the Wyoming legislature, became governor of Wyoming, and served as a U.S. senator from Wyoming until his death in 1933.

One interesting tidbit of history is the stained-glass window in the northeast corner of the St. Peter's Episcopal Church in Sheridan, Wyoming. In 1958, Manville Kendrick, John B. Kendrick's son, was asked to sponsor the window, which featured the Good Shepherd

---

[7] Beach, *Faded Hoof Prints—Bygone Dreams*, Maude Beach interview.

[8] Beach, *Faded Hoof Prints—Bygone Dreams*, Maude Beach interview.

[9] Beach, *Faded Hoof Prints—Bygone Dreams*, Selway Family story.

with a crook and three sheep. Kendrick responded that he would gladly sponsor the window in memory of his father, but:

No sheep! Replace the sheep with cows.

Replace the crook with a straight staff.

And so it was done. It certainly is good to be the king! The window is shown below.[10]

Figure 37: Stained-glass window on the northeast corner of St. Peter's Episcopal Church in Sheridan.

---

10 *Stained Glass Windows*, St. Peter's Episcopal Church pamphlet, Sheridan, Wyoming, and interview with Melinda Greenough, St. Peter's trustee.

THE PAST IN REVIEW

The Kendrick/Bear Creek Raid was a successful use of force and intimidation. It is a fascinating study in how power, loyalty, money, and force of personality can combine to influence the course of history. Kendrick, Howes, and Brewster were all men of power, vision, and action, as was Selway. This clash of titans was a memorable and historically important event. It was the largest number of sheep killed in a single raid in Montana history. It also marked the end of the open range era and the use of vigilantism to enforce Montana range customs and norms. While this raid was successful, it may have inadvertently encouraged later raids in Wyoming, which were less successful in the new century.

Had the raid taken place a year later, the outcome may have been completely different. February 1901 was the effective date that Montana's Rosebud County split off from Custer County and a new county attorney, sheriff, and board of county commissioners was named. One of the Rosebud County commissioners was Freeman Philbrick, a prominent sheep man who had himself been threatened by cattlemen.[1] Since the kill site was located very close to the new county, a "sheep-friendly" sheriff in Rosebud may have

---

[1] Brown and Felton, *Before Barbed Wire.*

pushed for a different investigation than the "cattle-friendly" O. C. Cato from Custer County.

Probably more important to the outcome than the county officials was the community respect accorded the planners and organizers of the raid. They had been careful not to injure any people, from the sheepherder to Daut and his wife. The public perception of the raid was that an unscrupulous sheep man (Selway) had tried to "pull a fast one" and had been slapped down. Also, the generous accommodation accorded to John Daut—payment for his sheep and improvements, allowed an extra year to move his flocks and and find fresh range on the Powder River—served to mitigate what otherwise could have been a public relations disaster.

Nonetheless, the raid was an unlawful act and the participants subject to prosecution. The fact that no one on the cattlemen side of the fight ever talked about the raid until all the others were dead was a tribute to the organizers and a measure of the respect the planners and participants had for each other, as well as the threat of violence against squealing.

One interesting fact is that three of the four Kendrick men who participated in the raid left employment of the OW and went out on their own within a year. Only "Tug" Wilson stayed with the OW until his death. Bill Munson, Walt Snider, and Frank McKinney all took up homesteads away from the Kendrick range, but continued to stay in the area. Did John B. Kendrick pay off these men to keep quiet? Probably not overtly. However, Kendrick demanded and expected loyalty from his employees. It would not be out of character for him to help his erstwhile employees with favorable terms from his position at the First National Bank of Sheridan or by the purchase of cattle or hay. The former employees would not have wanted to make an enemy of Kendrick or implicate themselves for their actions. It was rumored that Bill Munson's family credited John B. Kendrick's help in securing their irrigated ranch on the Tongue River. Walt Snider was given a favorable lease on the "Ceded Strip" on the Crow Reservation, and Frank McKinney secured a homestead on the Tongue River, ranches at Kirby and

Squirrel Creek, Montana, and a herd of cattle in a very short time. All three became successful cattlemen in their own right. Can it be assumed that one hand washed the other? As noted earlier in this account:

It is good to be the king, *and* one of the king's men.

Thank you for your interest in this story.

1900 United States Federal Census, State of Montana, Custer County, School District 01, District 0206. Census taken June 1900. National Archives and Records Administration.

Alderson, Irving, Jr. Interview with Forest Dunning, 2018. Personal recollections of Forest Dunning, on file at the Wyoming Room of the Sheridan County Fulmer Public Library.

Atkins, Patti. *Reflections of the Inn: Historic Sheridan Inn, House of 69 Gables*. Printed by Hawks Press, 1994.

Badgett, Wally. Interview with Forest Dunning, May 10, 2018. Personal recollections of Forest Dunning, on file at the Wyoming Room of the Sheridan County Fulmer Public Library.

Beach, Maude (compiler), Robert L. Thaden, Jr., ed. *Faded Hoof Prints—Bygone Dreams*. Published by the Powder River Historical Society, 1989.

Brewster, Lyman. "December 1900: The Quiet Slaughter." *Montana: The Magazine of Western History* 24, no. 1 (Winter 1974): 82–84.

Brown, Joseph, Jr. Conversations with Forest Dunning, summer 1964. Personal recollections of Forest Dunning, on file at the Wyoming Room of the Sheridan County Fulmer Public Library.

Brown, Mark H., and W. R. Felton. *Before Barbed Wire*. New York: Bramhall House Publishing, 1956.

Caddel, John Hudson "Shorty" (obituary). *The Sheridan Press*, May 23, 1966.

Caddel, John Hudson "Shorty." Conversation with John Moreland and Forest Dunning, 1956. Personal recollections of Forest Dunning, on file at the Wyoming Room of the Sheridan County Fulmer Public Library.

Caddel, John Hudson (Shorty). Transcript of interview with Robert Helvey. American Heritage Center, Robert Helvey Collection.

Cox, Maime "Peachy" Taylor. Interview with Floyd Alderson for the "Montanans at Work" Project, Montana Historical Society, 1969.

"Daut, John." One-page Range Riders Museum biography. Author unknown. The Papers of Dola Wilson and Charles M. Boucher (1936–1954).

Davis, John W. *A Vast Amount of Trouble.* Norman: University of Oklahoma Press, 1993.

Davis, John W. *Goodbye, Judge Lynch: The End of a Lawless Era in Wyoming's Big Horn Basin.* Norman: University of Oklahoma Press, 2005.

Dunning, Leota Kimes. Transcript of interview with Bob Helvey. American Heritage Center, Robert Helvey Collection, February 17, 1960.

Echoing Footsteps. Powder River County Extension Homemakers Council. Butte, MT: Ashton Printing & Engraving Company, 1967.

Goergen, Cynde A. *One Cowboy's Dream. John B. Kendrick: His Family, Home and Ranching Empire.* Virginia Beach, VA: The Donning Company Publishers, 1995.

"Gone on His Last Roundup." Author unknown. *Billings Gazette.* October 31, 1902.

Greenough, Melinda. Interview with Forest Dunning, 2018. Personal recollections of Forest Dunning, on file at the Wyoming Room of the Sheridan County Fulmer Public Library.

Hayes, Arthur, Jr. Interview with Forest Dunning, March 2018. Personal recollections of Forest Dunning, on file at the Wyoming Room of the Sheridan County Fulmer Public Library.

Howes, Levi. *Montana Territory.* Published by the author, date unknown.

In the Matter of the Will and Estate of Horton S. Boal, Rosebud County, Montana. Probate Case Number 21.

Kelly, Charles. *The Outlaw Trail: A History of Butch Cassidy and the Wild Bunch.* Lincoln: University of Nebraska Press (Bison Books Edition), 1938.

Kendrick, Rosa-Maye. Excerpts of diaries: "Stories from My Father." Sheridan County Fulmer Public Library.

King, Bucky. *The Empire Builders: The Development of the Kendrick Cattle Company*. Published by the author, 1992.

Lacy, Frank (Booker). Transcript of interview with Robert Helvey, American Heritage Center, Robert Helvey Collection.

McKinney, William. Interview with Forest Dunning, 2018. Personal recollections of Forest Dunning, on file at the Wyoming Room of the Sheridan County Fulmer Public Library.

Munson, William (obituary). *The Sheridan Press*, January 8, 1951.

"Report is Verified." Author unknown. *Forsyth Times*, January 8, 1901.

"Result of Range Trouble." *The Sheridan Post*, January 3, 1901.

Stained Glass Windows. Pamphlet published by St. Peter's Episcopal Church of Sheridan Wyoming.

State of Montana v. John B. Kendrick, District Court Case #367, Seventh Judicial District, Custer County, 1906 (partial records). Other records available under "R.R. Selway Suit," The Papers of John B. Kendrick, American Heritage Center, Laramie, Wyoming.

Stevens, Marcus. Interview with Forest Dunning, July 2018. Personal recollections of Forest Dunning, on file at the Wyoming Room of the Sheridan County Fulmer Public Library.

Thex, Neil. Interviews and correspondence with Forest Dunning, 2016–2018. Personal recollections of Forest Dunning, on file at the Wyoming Room of the Sheridan County Fulmer Public Library.

They Came and They Stayed. Rosebud County Bi-Centennial Committee. Billings, MT: Western Printing and Lithography, 1977.

"Wool Growers in Session." Author unknown. *The Yellowstone Journal*, April 17, 1901.

Forest B. Dunning is a retired rancher living in Sheridan, Wyoming. Raised in Birney, Montana, near the Northern Cheyenne Indian Reservation, he has been a student, cowboy, soldier, financial advisor, purebred cattle rancher, cattle buyer, and author. He is a graduate from New Mexico State University with a bachelor's degree in Agricultural Economics and from the U.S. Army Command and General Staff College with a master's degree in Military Science. After successful careers as a U.S. Army officer (retired lieutenant colonel) and a civilian financial advisor, Forest returned to his roots and bought a cattle ranch near Sheridan, Wyoming. He has long had a love for Montana and Wyoming history and historical fiction. Noting that much of local history had been overlooked, he has devoted his writing skills to the preservation of history in southeastern Montana, northern Wyoming, and the Northern Cheyenne Tribe.